Financial Care for Your Aging Parent

Financial Care for Your Aging Parent

Lise Andreana, CFP, CPCA

Self-Counsel Press
(a division of)
International Self-Counsel Press Ltd.
USA   Canada

Self-Counsel Press acknowledges the financial support of the Government of Canada through the Canada Book Fund for our publishing activities.

Printed in Canada.

First edition: 2014

Library and Archives Canada Cataloguing in Publication

Andreana, Lise, author
    Financial care for your aging parents / Lise Andreana.

(Eldercare series)
Issued in print and electronic formats.
ISBN 978-1-77040-192-1 (pbk.).—ISBN 978-1-77040-942-2 (epub).—
ISBN 978-1-77040-943-9 (kindle)

    1. Aging parents—Finance, Personal. 2. Adult children of aging parents—Family relationships. I. Title. II. Series: Eldercare series

HG179.A628 2014   332.0240085   C2014-900536-9
                                               C2014-900537-7

Self-Counsel Press
(a division of)
International Self-Counsel Press Ltd.

Bellingham, WA   North Vancouver, BC
USA   Canada

Contents

Worksheets

Notice to Readers

Laws are constantly changing. Every effort is made to keep this publication as current as possible. However, the author, the publisher, and the vendor of this book make no representations or warranties regarding the outcome or the use to which the information in this book is put and are not assuming any liability for any claims, losses, or damages arising out of the use of this book. The reader should not rely on the author or the publisher of this book for any professional advice. Please be sure that you have the most recent edition.

Note: The fees and taxes quoted in this book are correct at the date of publication. However, fees are subject to change without notice. For current fees, please check with the court registry or appropriate government office nearest you.

Prices, commissions, fees, and other costs mentioned in the text or shown in samples in this book probably do not reflect real costs where you live. Inflation and other factors, including geography, can cause the costs you might encounter to be much higher or even much lower than those we show. The dollar amounts shown are simply intended as representative examples.

Dedication

Anita & Peter:

*Know that my love for you is as strong as yours is for your children.
I have worked all my life to clear the road ahead, and move
obstacles to the side, so your load may be lighter. Keep this
book close at hand for one day you will need it.*

Love Mom

*To Victoria Hughes, my heartfelt appreciation for your help in
bringing order, clarity, and structure to my ideas. Together we
have produced a book we can be proud of. Thank you.*

Introduction

By the year 2021, it is estimated that there will be 6.7 million seniors in Canada. By 2041, this number will grow to 9.2 million, meaning that one in four Canadians will be a senior.[1] The statistics for the United States show a similar growth pattern for the aging population with 55 million achieving senior status by the year 2020 — a 36 percent increase over the next decade. The driving force behind this growth is the well-known "Baby Boom" between 1946 and 1965 that saw a dramatic increase in the number of children being born during that period.

With the fastest growing segment of the senior population being those older than age 85, and knowing that 70 percent of Boomers still have at least one living parent, that means many of the Boomer generation will be faced with the prospect of caring for their aging parents right at the same time they are approaching their own

1 "Becoming a CPCA: Core Concepts, Definitions & Practice Questions," Certified Professional Consultant on Aging (CPCA) www.cpcacanada.com.

retirement. Clearly, Boomers are headed for a crisis; one they may not have anticipated.

As our society moves away from institutional care, more seniors are staying in their homes and/or being cared for by family members. Almost 50 percent of seniors suffer from a disability. Even more shockingly, more than 80 percent are suffering from a chronic health condition.

Currently, more than 90 percent of caregiving in Canada is provided by either a family member or friend. The impact this role can have on caregivers can be as simple as missing out on socializing with other family and friends to more significant consequences such as fatigue, sleepless nights, and emotional or financial stress. Caregivers may also suffer lost wages due to time missed at work, as it is estimated that it costs Canadian businesses $16 billion a year when employees take time off to care for a loved one. This missed time can also result in losing out on opportunities for promotion, a reduction in savings capacity for their own retirement plans, and smaller pension plan amounts after being forced to retire early.

As aging parents face diminishing health — both physical and mental — it becomes increasingly more challenging to work with them to understand their financial situation and their personal wishes for living arrangements and care, and to protect their interests. Difficult emotions often come into play. Disagreements with siblings are common. Finding all their relevant legal and financial documents can feel overwhelming.

This book aims to provide you with the tools you need to —

- prepare for the possibility of taking on a caregiving role,
- balance your own retirement needs with those of your aging parents,
- create a sustainable financial plan for your parents,
- find resources that provide the services you may need (some at reduced costs),
- track your parents' finances,
- prepare for and select a retirement facility, and
- assist your parents with the sale of their home.

There is no time like the present to begin preparing for your aging parents' financial future. Being proactive can help minimize a great deal of stress and uncertainty down the road — for your parents, yourself, and your entire family.

The worksheets in this book are included in a download kit so that you may modify them to suit your needs at www.self-counsel.com/updates/financialcare/14forms.htm.

chapter 1

Preparing to Be a Caregiver

Not long ago, a treasured client of mine, Grace[1], had missed three appointments at our office. She completely forgot about the appointments the first two times they were scheduled. The third time we rescheduled, my associate called to remind her, but she got lost on her way to the office. I booked a fourth meeting, this time at her house.

I was concerned about her, so during our meeting I asked if she would give me permission to call her two daughters, Linda and Mary, and share some information with them. She signed a letter I had brought with me, giving me her permission.

Tellingly, as we had our discussion, she could not recall Mary's last name or telephone number. I called Linda and requested a joint meeting with her and her sister, and explained (without going into detail) that I had some concerns about her mother's health.

1 Names and case details have been changed to protect the clients.

The meeting went well, and at the end of our discussion outlining my concerns, I suggested two things:

1. Grace needed to update her will and power of attorney.
2. An appointment needed to be made for her to see a gerontologist.

Grace did both. The lawyer's meeting came first, and they were able to complete the power of attorney and will with her. The gerontologist appointment came later, and confirmed my concerns: Grace was diagnosed with Alzheimer's disease.

Grace's story is not unique, and the steps her daughters have had to take since then are becoming more common. Her daughters are part of what we refer to as the "sandwich generation." Recent trends show kids in their twenties are choosing to stay in the family home longer, leaving Boomers fearing that when they finally have a freshly emptied nest, they will be faced with taking on their own aging parents who will then require full-time care.

Your best years should be from retirement — generally between the ages of 60 to 80, and up to the onset of chronic illness. Yet, according to the Certified Professional Consultant on Aging (CPCA), these are the years where you are most likely to be called on to help with aging parents.

But wait a minute! Aren't these the "golden years" you've been dreaming about? The years of travel and adventure, free from worry? Your children are grown and out of the house, and you get to enjoy the freedom from responsibility for others, right?

Most of us love our parents and have a sense of responsibility for them, so we want to do the right thing when it comes to their care. As Amy Adams' character said in the movie *Trouble with the Curve* when her father (played by Clint Eastwood) asked why she was still there trying to help him through his health problems, "I feel this dysfunctional sense of responsibility to make sure that you're okay." If, like Amy, you are worried about your aging parents and their ability to care for themselves, this book is for you!

Are you wondering when is the right time to get help for your parents? Are you struggling with what the best time is to move them from home care to a long-term care facility? These are tough questions for any child to answer. I have often teased my own children that I want to get a tattoo with a "best before date" in big, bold letters, clearly instructing them on when it is the right time to place my infirm remains in a nice, warm, comfortable retirement residence at the first sign of senility. If only it were that easy.

This book is designed to help you balance the needs of your aging parents with your own lifestyle needs and retirement dreams.

1. The Different Stages of the Elderly

There are different stages of being a senior; people can be distinguished between the Youthful, Middle Age, and Elderly of the senior years.

Youthful seniors are represented by those who are healthy and active — typically between the ages of 65 and 75 (or older, if still in good health). These are the years of high activity, sometimes including continued work, travel, and even extreme sports. These are frequently also the caregivers of their chronically ill parents.

Seniors in their *Middle Years*, older than age 75, are still active but to a lesser degree. They may be suffering from a chronic illness, which limits their activities to a certain extent. They still have the ability to live independent lives, and most choose to remain living in their own homes. Indeed, they are encouraged to do so by society and by our government agencies, until the onset of a serious critical illness, or if and when they are no longer able to perform what are known as The Activities of Daily Life[2].

The Activities of Daily Life consist of the following:

- Eating and feeding ourselves
- Dressing ourselves
- Bathing ourselves and maintaining basic hygiene and toilet activities without help
- Transferring in and out of bed, bath, or chair without help
- Maintaining our home and surroundings for basic cleanliness and safety

Once a chronic illness interferes with an older senior's ability to carry on independently, we refer to them as *Elderly*. This has more to do with ability than actual age. For example, there are many highly active and engaged individuals older than 80 who would rarely be referred to as "elderly"; for example, Warren Buffett, Queen Elizabeth, Sir Michael Caine, Betty White, and Maya Angelou.

---

2 "Activites of Daily Life (ADLs) and Instrumental Activities of Daily Life (IADLs)," Senior Housing Net, accessed January 20, 2014.
www.seniorhousingnet.com/assisted-living/adlsandiadls.aspx?source=web

As mentioned in the introduction, the North American population is aging at a remarkable rate thanks in part to the number of births in the Baby Boom generation, continued advances in medicine, and healthy lifestyles. By the year 2041 we will see one in every four persons qualify as a senior. With the fastest growing segment of the senior population being those older than 85, it is more likely than ever before that Youthful seniors will be taking care of their parents in the Elderly senior category.

In the USA, the Administration on Aging (www.aoa.gov) gives the following statistics:

- Of the US population, 1 in 8 is 65 years or older.

- Population of those older than the age 65 numbered 40.4 million people in 2010.

- Expected population of 65-year-olds by 2020 is 55 million, and by 2030, it is expected the number will grow to 72.1 million.

- It is estimated that between 20 to 40 percent of US adults are now caring for a sick or an elderly family member. Since most caregivers are family, accurate data is difficult to come by.

- The US economy is cited as a cause for more sick and elderly being cared for at home by informal caregivers (mostly family members).

The Certified Professional Consultant on Aging (CPCA) cites the following Canadian statistics in their course material "Becoming a CPCA":

- 1 in 5 Canadians age 45 and older are providing care to a senior.

- 6 percent of Canadians older than age 75 report being caregivers.

- Adults have more parents than children for the first time in history

A recent Statistics Canada report identifies 8 million Canadians as caregivers in 2012[3], and the number one reason cited for requiring caregiving in this report was *aging* (28 percent). Adding Alzheimer's and dementia to that number (an additional 6 percent) shows that almost 3 million people are already caring for our aging population. It's time to get prepared.

---

3 "Portrait of Caregivers, 2012," Statistics Canada, accessed January 20, 2014. www.ccc-ccan.ca/media.php?mid=378

2. Why Do We Fear Aging?

In my more than 20 years of experience as a Certified Financial Planner, working with more than 1,000 Boomers, they are, by and large, working toward their retirement savings goals. However, the majority are behind in their required saving schedule, which presents a serious problem. At best, most are on target to retire at 75 percent of their retirement goal. This may require accepting a reduced retirement lifestyle, or working longer (delaying retirement) in order to achieve the savings needed for their desired retirement lifestyle.

As Boomers prepare to retire, they are increasingly being faced with the onset of chronic illness and infirmity of their aging parents. In my experience, Boomers feel obligated to help out, often at a cost to their current lifestyle, and ultimately their retirement lifestyle as well. These costs will be both financial and social.

Taking on the responsibility for the financial care of your aging parents at the same time you are planning your own retirement presents a unique set of challenges. For many of you this may mean a loss of time and money from work, forced early retirement, or a loss of freedom within your own retirement to pursue those long-held and cherished retirement dreams.

In my experience with my own family and my clients, most elderly parents are being less than forthright about their diminishing capabilities. This is a scary time for them, and there are many reasons why they may be withholding information from their adult children:[4]

- Fear of losing independence and treasured privacy.
- Fear of acknowledging mortality.
- Fearing the change of new surroundings, new routines, and new people.
- Not wanting to burden loved ones with their care.
- Fear of the cost of any treatments or care they may require.
- Embarrassment in admitting they can no longer perform certain tasks.
- They may already be experiencing dementia or mental health issues that prevent them from knowing what is happening to them or recognizing their limitations.

---

4 "Caring for the Elderly: Dealing with resistance," Mayo Clinic, accessed January 20, 2014. www.mayoclinic.com/health/caring-for-the-elderly/MY01436

As their child, you may be scared as well, causing you to miss the signs of diminished capacity. Common reasons adult children do not see the signs include:

- Not wanting to admit a parent is getting older and may be approaching death.
- Fear of having an emotional and/or confrontational conversation with the parent.
- Fear of having to take on the financial, emotional, and social costs of caregiving.
- Fear of not knowing what steps to take next.
- Fear of the impact caregiving will have on their marriage, job, and life.

These fears and concerns are common and valid. Caring for your aging parents takes time. If you are still working and raising a family, this is likely to be time you don't have. Caring for your aging parents may also impact your own financial resources.

If you are reading this book and asking yourself if it is time to step in and help your aging parents, I can assure you that if you are asking that question, the answer is "yes"! It is never too early for a parent or adult child to begin a conversation of "what if," and to plan for the day when complete independence is no longer a viable option.

3. How Do You Know Your Loved One Needs Help?

As a financial planner to retirees for more than 20 years, on more than one occasion I have asked my clients for permission to speak to their adult children, just like I did with Grace in the story mentioned at the beginning of this chapter. The purpose of those calls was to let their children know that I had reason to be concerned about their parents' abilities. Missed appointments and getting lost on the way to our office are just some of the things that may point to a larger, underlying problem. Forgetting the name of their son-in-law or grandchild may be signs of a larger problem. By getting our clients' children involved, we have helped some of our clients receive testing for, and confirm a diagnosis of, early stage Alzheimer's.

If you are still unsure if it is time to step in, let's help you identify where you are.

Gerontology specialists use two main measures when evaluating whether a person needs outside help and intervention. The first are the Activities of Daily Life mentioned earlier in section **1.** If your loved one has problems with the following activities, then intervention is required:

- Incontinence
- Eating, and feeding oneself
- Getting in and out of bed
- Toileting
- Bathing
- Dressing
- Safety

The second list of activities, known as Instrumental or Intermediate Activities of Daily Life, are also essential when living alone:

- Managing finances
- Using the telephone
- Shopping
- Preparing meals
- Housekeeping
- Doing laundry
- Driving or using transportation
- Managing medications

Keep in mind, if your parents cannot maintain all the activities listed, that doesn't necessarily mean they can no longer live independently in their own home; it just means they will require some support in order to do so for the time being.

While it may seem like the inability to do any of these tasks would be easy to spot, remember that it is difficult to notice many of these challenges unless you are living with the person. Simply asking for updates on the phone may not be sufficient as your parents may not want to worry you with the truth if they are having trouble. Acknowledge that as their child, you may not want to hear the truth yet either, as it means you will have to face some potentially scary health information about your loved one, as well as need to step in and take action. As scary as the truth may be, the sooner you know, the better.

Getting an honest picture of how your parents are doing requires a bit of detective work. Here are some things to look for the next time you visit their home:

- Observe how well they are dressed and their personal hygiene, especially when compared to how they typically looked in the past.

- Check the fridge and look into the level of food they keep on hand, and compare that with how frequently they are able to get to the store for more. Is it enough?

- Ask to see where they keep their medication. Compare the number of tablets in each bottle with the date the prescription was filled and ensure it is depleting at the correct rate.

- Make sure bills are being paid by checking for overdue notices, and seeing whether the phone, television, and electricity are all in working order.

- Check on levels of things such as laundry and garbage, and the cleanliness of their clothing, rooms, and bedding.

- Check that major changes haven't happened without you knowing, such as the loss of their driver's license, falls or injuries, or instances of getting lost.

- Ask for details about their social activities and take note of any social withdrawal behavior, such as no longer playing cards with friends or other activities they used to do regularly.

- Take note of any memory issues they exhibit, such as forgetting names of grandchildren or friends during conversation.

- Ask about their health. Sometimes they might not want to burden you with bad news, but if you ask a direct question about any new conditions they might have, or whether they've had to make any recent trips to the doctor, they'll be more likely to tell you.

4. Are You Ready to Be a Caregiver?

Given the likelihood of you or your spouse taking on caregiving responsibilities at some point in the future, it is helpful to consider your readiness in doing so as early as possible. Whether or not the role of caregiver is taken on by choice or out of necessity, one of the most important things to consider and be aware of is the impact such a role will have on your life.

While caregivers can enjoy a great sense of satisfaction and purpose in knowing they are helping a loved one, there are challenges to be aware of including:[5]

- Financial stress
- Loss of social life
- Giving up personal interests due to lack of time or money
- Emotional stress including anxiety, loss of appetite, and depression
- Behavioral stresses such as dealing with challenging family dynamics and loss of privacy

Examining the full scope of a caregiver role is helpful in understanding what you can do ahead of time to prepare. Worksheet 1 can help gauge your readiness and point you towards the questions you need to start asking. (This Worksheet is in the download kit so you can print a copy or complete it on your computer using MS Word or compatible software.)

If your answer is "no" to any of these questions, it is time to take action and start preparing. Fortunately, you have already taken a big step in reading this book. Don't be afraid. The answers and preparations you need are in your hands right now! Preparation doesn't need to be overwhelming, and the earlier you start, the better. By following the action plan that comes next, you can do a lot to get ready.

5. The Seven-Step Action Plan for Caregivers

If you are entering into a caregiver role, or simply want to start preparing for the possibility, the following seven-step action plan will help you get started, clarify the steps you need to take, and outline key points you need to explore. Many of these steps are outlined in more detail throughout this book, with additional tools to help you through this process.

1. **Educate yourself about caregiving and the health-care system:** Look for books on caregiving in your local library, helpful articles and websites online (there are many), and reach out to other caregivers you may know to get their advice and perspective. Touch base with your local community care action center or community support services to find out what services are available in your community to serve the needs of seniors.

---

5 "Caregiver Compass," accessed January 20, 2014. "www.saintelizabeth.com/getmedia/1dd53c40-d187-45e8-bd83-d587efd08b83/Caregiver-Compass-Online.pdf.aspx

Worksheet 1
Determine Your Readiness to be a Caregiver

1. Have you acknowledged that there is a high likelihood that you will be required to act as a caregiver one or more times in your life? This may be for an aging parent and possibly a spouse or common-law partner.

2. Do you know what is involved in being a caregiver for someone who requires 24/7 care? Could you list off all the activities and responsibilities involved?

3. Have you built this caregiving role into your financial and retirement plans, knowing that there is a likelihood that it will happen when you are in your own retirement years and that it could last for an extended period of time?

4. Are your own legal and financial documents updated and in order?

5. Are you aware of the costs attached to care, from in-home caregiver fees to the equipment costs and potential home safety and accessibility modifications that may be necessary?

6. Are you aware of the different types of government- and community-based services that exist to help with caregiving? Do you know how to access them and apply for the services?

7. Do you have backup plans in your retirement planning in case you need to leave the workforce earlier than expected to care for a loved one?

8. Have you considered the impact caregiving would have on your social and lifestyle expectations and your own plans for retirement if you are required to take on that role?

9. Have you built in adequate financial plans for your own caregiving requirements during retirement so that when you reach a stage that requires full-time care you will not need to impose any costs on your children or loved ones?

10. Have you discussed caregiving wishes with your parents and spouse so that you feel comfortable that you clearly know their wishes and expectations for care?

Be prepared for the losses your parents may face and how you may have to deal with them, including incontinence, memory loss, wandering, and inability to recognize you or other loved ones. The more you know, the fewer surprises you'll be faced with later.

2. **Get to know the financial and tax support available:** There are many tax benefits and government programs aimed at assisting those in caregiving roles and helping to minimize the financial burden involved. (See section **6.** for more information.)

3. **Get organized:** Find the documentation you will need to fulfill this role. This means ensuring your parents' will and power of attorney forms are completed, up to date, and easy to find. Ensure any financial documents related to bills, pensions, insurance, and investments are also up to date and well organized, with key contact information and account numbers provided in case you need assistance.

4. **Stay organized:** Once caregiving begins, create a "Care Binder" (hard copy or via a shared online document) to house all the relevant information you and your family will need to maintain care for your loved one. Fill it with things such as schedules of upcoming appointments, medical information on types of medications and when they'll need refilling, contact information for close neighbors and friends, and notes on any changes you notice in your parent, good or bad, that will be helpful to share with doctors and loved ones. Always take a list of questions and a pen and paper with you to medical appointments so that you can be sure to get all the information you need to adequately care for your loved one. Don't leave the appointment until you have all those answers written down for future reference and clarification.

5. **Communicate:** Ask the questions that will help you understand the true wishes of your aging parents. Before you can truly make plans and budgets, you need to understand what type of care they are hoping for and where. Having realistic discussions about the cost of different facility options is essential. Ensure that all family members are aware of the wishes of the person who will need care, what the plan is, what different stages and related timing are likely to be involved, and that everyone is willing and able to take on their

part in the plan. Make sure all siblings know who is going to be the power of attorney and what that entails.

While communicating, avoid making promises you may not be able to keep. If, for example, your parent asks you to promise to never place him or her in a nursing home, it may be more realistic to tell him or her you'll do the best you can to avoid it, but if health and safety concerns make it the best option down the road, you need the flexibility to do what is best for them.

6. **Create a budget for care:** Research the costs of the different stages of care and ensure that adequate funds will be ready and accessible at those times. Partner with your parent's financial planner to make this happen properly so any delays, surprises, or obstacles will be avoided.

7. **Create a plan to care for the caregiver:** In order to be an effective caregiver, you need to take care of yourself as well. You will need to take breaks to replenish and recharge your physical and emotional energy, so ensure you are building a plan to do so by having other people you can rely on when you need a break, and by making time for activities that you find enjoyable. Taking respite from your caregiving duties will prevent burnout. Enrolling your loved one in an adult day program is one option for respite, as is having someone else come to the home to perform some caregiving duties instead of you (some can be arranged for free by getting a referral by a doctor). For longer breaks, you can pay for your parent to have a short-term stay in a long-term facility.

You will also benefit from talking to other caregivers (in person or in online support groups) to help remind you that you are not alone on this challenging journey.

6. Benefits and Tax Supports Available to Caregivers

There are many benefits and tax supports available to caregivers. Read on for more information:

- **Tax credits for caregivers:** In the US, there are some tax credits provided by the government. Some of these benefits include deducting contributions a child made by claiming his or her parent as a dependent. This tax benefit can be used for deducting money a taxpayer paid towards his or her parents' medical care and expenses. You can find more information by contacting the Internal Revenue Service (IRS) for Publication 502: Medical and Dental Expenses.

In Canada, under the Disability Tax Credit and the Medical Expense Tax Credit, you may be eligible for tax credits. If you are maintaining a home for an eligible dependent relative, you may also be able to claim the Caregiver Tax Credit as well, unless the person is your spouse or common-law partner. As of time of this book's publication, there was also an additional Family Caregiver Tax Credit. More detailed information can be found on the Canada Revenue Agency (CRA) website.

- **Personal emergency leave:** Details for this benefit allowing you to take time off from your job may vary by jurisdiction, so it is best to check with your local government office for more details.

- **Compassionate Care Benefit Program:** This benefit is offered via Service Canada and more detailed information on qualifying and applying can be found on the Service Canada website.

- **Family and medical leave:** This is an unpaid, job-protected leave to provide care for a loved one who faces a life-threatening illness. Details and conditions vary by jurisdiction, so again, it is essential to check with your local government office for specific details.

- **Attendant Care:** You may be able to claim a partial or even full amount for a parent in a full-time nursing home, or the salary you pay to an attendant who cares for a parent in your home.

It's also important to be smart about who claims what when it comes to tax time. Splitting caregiving costs and seeking tax breaks between spouses may have better tax advantages than doing it via one person's tax return. Getting advice from a financial or tax planner on this can help maximize your tax savings.

7. Caregiving Will Change Your Life

There are many ways your life will change if you step into the role of caregiver, especially if you assume a caregiving role from within your own home when a parent comes to live with you. Your job, finances, and social life will be impacted. Your ability to travel, your emotional well-being, and your retirement dreams will be impacted. That sounds like a lot, but know that with good planning, that impact will feel far less overwhelming.

Remember that despite the challenges, there is a great feeling of satisfaction in knowing you are taking care of a loved one and helping him or her make the most of his or her later years in a safe and loving environment.

Another of my cherished clients, Dawn, went through this care-giving process with her mother not so long ago. Her mother was diagnosed with pancreatic cancer, and while many patients with this diagnosis live less than 12 months, Dawn's mother lived another 5 years. Since Dawn was told of the short time frame expected, she willingly took on the full caregiving responsibilities for her mother, assuming that her mother did not have much longer to live.

While her mother enjoyed much better health in years three and four — thanks to remission and pain control — Dawn still experienced a lot of mental and physical fatigue in those five long years. Thankfully she had a very supportive husband who helped keep her from "losing it" or throwing in the towel, and little did they know that all the while, he was learning from her example and would use that knowledge to assist his own ailing mother shortly thereafter.

Finding a healthy balance between the rewards and the challenges can be done with awareness, diligent planning, and preparedness. There is still time to build a solid financial plan that will allow your parents to be taken care of in their home as long as possible, and in the facility of their choice, in the style and manner they wish, when the time eventually comes.

There is still time to ensure that your retirement dreams can come true as well. Most importantly, there's no time like the present to get started. In the next Chapter, we'll discuss how planning starts with *you* and your own retirement readiness.

chapter 2

Taking Care of Yourself First:
Preparing for Your Own Retirement

If you have ever been on a plane, you'll remember the many times you've watched the flight attendants demonstrate emergency procedures. One of the things they always remind us to do if the oxygen masks drop down from the ceiling is to put our own mask on first, before we tend to our children and loved ones. While it is often in our nature to feel that we should help our loved ones first, it can be dangerous to do so in this instance. This is because we can't help others breathe if we aren't breathing ourselves. The same is true when it comes to retirement planning. We must first safely set ourselves up for success before we will be in a position to help others.

You have an obligation to ensure you will be self-sufficient in your retirement years. This means balancing your own needs with those of your children and your aging parents.

1. Is It Time for You to Retire?

Just because you have reached a particular milestone, such as years of service or age, it does not mean you have to retire. If staying in the workforce is still rewarding — even for an extra year — it can give you great financial benefits, as well as provide rewarding mental and physical stimulation. However, it is important to consider what your retirement lifestyle dreams look like.

Today's active retirees may find they spend as much money (or more) during retirement as they did while working! The old-age stage has its expenses as well, such as moving to assisted-living residences or long-term care facilities. It's time to really think about your hopes and dreams, and make a list of the types of activities you want to participate in throughout your retirement, from travel, to dining out, to club memberships, and more.

In addition to lifestyle expenses, think about whether you will be financially supporting a spouse or an adult child at the time of your retirement. As we've discussed already, there may be a likelihood that you will need to help your aging parents if they do not have sufficient funds.

Theravive, a network of counselors and clinics throughout North America, estimates that 33 percent of adult children who are caring for their aging parents are either retired or work part time.[1] This means by financially helping others, it will have a dramatic impact on your income needs.

No matter what age you are now, it's not too late to save adequately for retirement. The following sections list helpful tips to get you started.

1.1 Tips for 50-year olds

If you haven't yet given serious consideration to your retirement, now is the time. At age 50, there is still time to plan and save for retirement during the next 10 to 15 years. With children now leaving the family nest, and careers in full bloom, expenses are lower and income is on the rise. This is the time to take advantage and reduce your debt as well as increase your retirement account savings.

---

1 Accessed January 20, 2014. www.theravive.com

1.1a Tip 1: Paying down debt

It is very difficult to enjoy retirement when a large portion of your fixed income will go to servicing debt — especially debt accumulated during the working years! Pay off debt with the highest interest rates first, such as credit cards. Did you know that over one year, a $5,000 credit card balance with an 18 percent interest rate (a typical rate for a credit card) would cost you $900 in interest?

Once your consumer debt is paid off, it is time to reduce or pay off the remaining mortgage you have on your home or cottage.

1.1b Tip 2: Start saving

Your 50s are the ideal time to top up your registered retirement accounts (e.g., Registered Retired Savings Plans and Tax-Free Savings Accounts). This is especially true if your earnings are near their peak, since those higher earnings are taxed at a higher income tax rate!

1.1c Tip 3: Protect your family

With the children grown and gone, debt paid off, and savings accounts in good shape, you may think there is no need for insurance. Unfortunately, aging often leads to illness. Consideration should be given to two types of insurance: Critical Illness Insurance and Long-Term Care Insurance.

- Critical Illness Insurance pays a lump sum to the insured party 30 days after the diagnosis of one of a list of diseases, such as cancer, heart disease, and stroke. Coverage amounts can vary between $10,000 and $2,000,000. Proceeds from Critical Illness policies can be used in any way the insured party chooses, such as accessing high-priced health-care treatments, paying down debt, or taking that once-in-a-lifetime holiday.

- Long-Term Care Insurance helps cover the cost of long-term care, just as the name implies. This insurance pays a benefit when the insured party can no longer perform at least two of the main Activities of Daily Life (discussed in Chapter 1). The insured amount is paid monthly or weekly, and helps with the increased costs that disability can bring.

As with any insurance, it is best to engage a qualified financial planner to help you determine what coverage you need, and how much coverage is right for you and your family.

1.1d Tip 4: Spend money!

Once you have paid down your debt, topped up your savings account, and reviewed your insurance needs, don't be afraid to spend a little money and have some fun. Your fifties may be some of the best years of your life!

1.2 Tips for 60-year olds

You are officially a senior! You qualify for all kinds of discounts, and the local pub's Happy Hour may be your favorite way to spend the dinner hour. Now is the time to meet with your financial advisor and tax planner to look into the following tips.

1.2a Tip 1: Tax planning

It is important to take the time to understand the impact of your tax bracket. If retired, you can control where your income comes from. It is worth the effort to plan income sources in the most tax-efficient manner possible.

1.2b Tip 2: Tax credits

Keep in mind that you could be eligible for tax credits such as the personal exemption, age credit, and spousal amount. You may also qualify for disability, caregiver, and infirm dependent amounts too.

1.2c Tip 3: Income splitting

In Canada, the Federal Government now allows couples to split pension income that can dramatically reduce the family tax bill when one spouse has significantly higher pension income than his or her partner.

American readers should check with the person who prepares their income tax returns to discuss the possibility of income splitting. Each state deals with this differently.

1.2d Tip 4: Travel

Now that you are nearing retirement, or retired, visions of Freedom 55 (make that Freedom 65 for the modern couple) may be dancing in your head. If you dream of escaping the cold of Canada's winters, be aware that there can be serious tax implications for those who overstay their welcome in the USA. As a visitor to the USA for an extended period of time, you will be required to complete Form 8840 to prove you have a closer connection to Canada than the United States. Failing this test, you will be required to file an American tax return. Also, don't forget that if you are planning to travel for an extended period, you need to consider who will be taking care of any aging parents while you're away.

Don't forget to purchase emergency travel insurance before you leave. If you are a snowbird, you may want to check the price of extended travel insurance, as the annual rate can provide savings over purchasing your coverage for one trip at a time. If you rent a vehicle when you travel, call your auto and home insurer and ask if it offers collision and liability coverage on the vehicle you plan to rent while on holidays.

Now that you know the helpful tips to make sure you're on track, it's time to really put pen to paper and figure out if you'll be able to retire at the age you're hoping. Bear with me as we get into the math; as painful as it is sometimes, there is no better way to see how ready you are than by writing down the actual numbers. I promise I'll make it as simple and painless as possible! Let's begin by using Worksheet 2 to figure out whether or not you'll be able to retire on time. (You can find a blank copy of this worksheet in the download kit.)

Worksheet 2
Retirement Readiness

1. Calculate how much financial support you can expect to receive from the government.
2. Calculate how much you can expect from your employer.
3. Figure out how much you will need.
4. Calculate shortfalls.
5. Calculate your debts (and reduce or eliminate them before retirement).
6. Don't bet on an inheritance.

2. Five Retirement Lifestyle Budgets

Now that you have a good idea of your retirement income sources and the savings you will be able to accumulate before you retire, take a look at the five retirement lifestyles in the following sections to see which one most closely matches your situation. The budgets demonstrate how other retirees in your income bracket allocate their funds.

Note: The five budgets are based on Statistics Canada 2001 household expenditure averages and then adjusted to suit scenarios. These budgets are samples for educational purposes only. Personal taxes assume that partners are in the same income tax bracket.

2.1 Conservative

Sample 1 describes a lifestyle that provides a modest home or rental unit in a small city. Much of your time is spent with friends and family who live nearby. Leisure time is spent gardening, playing bridge, and going for walks. Vacations are modest.

2.2 Comfortable

Sample 2 outlines the comfortable lifestyle which affords a three-bedroom house in a medium-sized city. Free time — and some money — go toward working on local community affairs and charities. Leisure time pleasures include gardening, reading novels, entertaining at home or dining out with friends and family members. This year's trip is a one-week stay at a nearby resort.

2.3 Above average

Sample 3 shows a lifestyle that provides a three-bedroom house in a large city. Leisure time activities include gardening, reading novels, entertaining either at home or dining out with friends and family members. Hobbies include yoga or membership at the local community tennis courts. Renting an apartment on the sandy shores of Florida for a few weeks each year brings a reprieve from the long winter months.

2.4 Luxury

Sample 4 describes a lifestyle that enables time to be split between the long-time home in an upscale metropolitan suburb and a newly purchased condo in Florida. Leisure time is spent entertaining friends either at home or in restaurants, and with a club membership where you can enjoy tennis or golf. The big vacation this year is a two-week tour of southern France.

2.5 Prestige

Sample 5 shows a lifestyle that provides for three pieces of real estate that are owned free and clear of mortgages. They include a primary residence, cottage, and condo in the sunny south with all the

Sample 1
Conservative Lifestyle Budget

Item	Single	Couple
Food	$3,321	$5,084
Housing: Primary residence including property tax, insurance, and utilities	$5,744	$6,291
Household operations including maintenance and repairs	$2,790	$3,349
Clothing	$832	$1,252
Recreation and leisure (e.g., entertainment, TV, hobbies, sports, club memberships)	$633	$1,489
Travel	$650	$1,000
Transportation (e.g., vehicle, insurance, public transit, parking)	$3,157	$4,982
Health and personal care (e.g., hair styling, dry cleaning)	$1,650	$2,400
Gifts and donations	$1,255	$2,418
Tobacco and alcohol	$414	$685
Savings	$199	$851
Interest paid and miscellaneous	$277	$335
Estimated personal income taxes	$3,720	$5,729
Total Annual Income	**$24,642**	**$35,865**

Sample 2
Comfortable Lifestyle Budget

Item	Single	Couple
Food	$4,151	$6,863
Housing: Primary residence including property tax, insurance, and utilities	$7,467	$8,493
Household operations including maintenance and repairs	$3,627	$4,689
Clothing	$1,165	$2,191
Recreation and leisure (e.g., entertainment, TV, hobbies, sports, club memberships)	$1,108	$3,052
Travel	$1,300	$3,400
Transportation (e.g., vehicle, insurance, public transit, parking)	$4,736	$8,719
Health and personal care (e.g., hair styling, dry cleaning)	$2,475	$3,000
Gifts and donations	$2,008	$3,385
Tobacco and alcohol	$873	$1,161
Savings	$1,343	$2,128
Interest paid and miscellaneous	$536	$568
Estimated personal income taxes	$12,576	$13,439
Total Annual Income	**$43,365**	**$61,088**

Sample 3
Above-Average Lifestyle Budget

Item	Single	Couple
Food	$4,982	$7,893
Housing: Primary residence including property tax, insurance, and utilities	$9,334	$10,616
Household operations including maintenance and repairs	$4,534	$5,861
Clothing	$1,631	$2,848
Recreation and leisure (e.g., entertainment, TV, hobbies, sports, club memberships)	$1,662	$4,579
Travel	$2,730	$5,440
Transportation (e.g., vehicle, insurance, public transit, parking)	$6,630	$11,770
Health and personal care (e.g., hair styling, dry cleaning)	$3,094	$3,750
Gifts and donations	$2,610	$4,570
Tobacco and alcohol	$907	$1,451
Savings	$1,679	$4,361
Interest paid and miscellaneous	$738	$828
Estimated personal income taxes	$18,239	$31,506
Total Annual Income	**$58,770**	**$95,473**

Sample 4
Luxury Lifestyle Budget

Item	Single	Couple
Food	$5,380	$9,077
Housing: Primary residence including property tax, insurance, and utilities	$11,201	$14,862
Housing: Florida condo including property tax, insurance, and condo fees	$6,721	$8,917
Household operations for two properties, including maintenance and repairs	$6,347	$7,912
Clothing	$2,283	$4,272
Recreation and leisure (e.g., entertainment, TV, hobbies, sports, club memberships)	$2,326	$7,326
Travel	$3,822	$10,880
Transportation (e.g., vehicle, insurance, public transit, parking)	$9,282	$15,301
Health and personal care (e.g., hair styling, dry cleaning)	$3,867	$4,688
Gifts and donations	$4,829	$6,398
Tobacco and alcohol	$1,179	$2,004
Savings	$2,351	$4,798
Interest paid and miscellaneous	$1,126	$1,033
Estimated personal income taxes	$26,594	$45,617
Total Annual Retirement Income	**$87,308**	**$143,085**

Sample 5
Prestige Lifestyle Budget

Item	Single	Couple
Food	$5,810	$9,985
Housing: Primary residence including property tax, insurance, and utilities	$15,121	$22,294
Housing: Florida condo including property tax, insurance, and condo fees	$9,980	$14,714
Housing: Cottage property including taxes, insurance, and utilities	$12,097	$17,835
Household operations for three properties, including maintenance and repairs	$9,521	$10,681
Clothing	$3,425	$5,768
Recreation and leisure (e.g., entertainment, TV, hobbies, sports, club memberships)	$3,489	$9,890
Travel	$5,733	$14,688
Transportation (e.g., vehicle, insurance, public transit, parking)	$13,922	$20,656
Health and personal care (e.g., hair styling, dry cleaning)	$4,834	$6,328
Gifts and donations	$6,519	$9,597
Tobacco and alcohol	$1,532	$2,604
Savings	$3,526	$6,477
Interest paid and miscellaneous	$1,688	$1,395
Estimated personal income taxes	$36,999	$62,005
Total Annual Retirement Income	**$134,196**	**$214,917**

amenities for a break from the cold winters, and warmer months are spent at your lakefront summer home with a fantastic country club close by that offers golf, tennis, and swimming. Much of your time is spent with close friends, entertaining at home, in restaurants, or at the club. You'll enjoy a three-week European getaway including a spectacular cruise down the Rhine. Theater and the symphony are also passions you indulge.

Once you've thoroughly explored your own readiness, and set yourself up for financial success on retirement, we can get back to helping your aging parents prepare for the years ahead. In Chapter 3 we will explore the best way to get started when talking to your parents about their own wishes and needs.

Asking Your Parents the Right Questions

I can't stress enough that there is no time like the present to start asking questions. Your parents are not getting any younger and with age often comes increasing difficulty in communicating effectively. It's time to ask your parents for their input while they are still capable of providing sound answers.

The needs of the elderly can be summarized into three categories: health, social, and financial. This chapter will discuss each of these areas with an emphasis on planning, problem solving, and accessing help to avoid financial loss.

If you want additional insights into the best way to communicate with aging parents, I highly recommend the book *How to Say It to Seniors,* by David Solie (Prentice Hall Press, 2004). In my opinion, this is the best book yet on communicating with the elderly. Its key message is that the elderly fear a loss of control and independence in their lives. They know they are suffering from diminishing capacity, and they are afraid of losing control. This book provides excellent advice on how to talk to your elderly parents and engage them in change that will lead them to a safer and happier old age.

1. The Five Myths of Aging

Before you begin your conversation with your elderly parents, keep the following five myths of aging in mind. Remember, you'll be in their shoes one day too.

1. To be old is to be sick.
2. You can't teach an old dog new tricks.
3. The secret to successful aging is to choose your parents wisely.
4. The horse is out of the barn.
5. The elderly don't pull their own weight.

I would counter that, to be sick, will make you *feel* old. There are many elderly who live active, interesting lives and contribute to their communities. In fact, I have found the elderly similar to the rest of us, which is they want to be recognized for their contributions to society. They have demonstrated that when they are treated with respect and consideration they have the ability to adapt to changing circumstances. However, as they age, so many of these changes are out of their control.

2. Opening the Conversation with Your Loved One

If you remember from your teen years, your parents likely sat you down for the "money" talk. This may have been no more pleasant than the "other" talk many of us lived through. Now that you are all grown up, you have responsibilities and a family of your own. However, the last few times you visited your elderly parents, you noticed they are not as sharp and active as they used to be, and you know it is only a matter of time before they will need your help. Perhaps they already suffer from a chronic illness.

The gap between healthy life years in retirement and life expectancy is growing. With average life expectancy for men now at 78 years and women at 83, we have to think realistically about how many of those years will be healthy and active. As discussed earlier in this book, we expect the healthy years to last through the mid-70s to mid-80s. That implies that, on average, your elderly parents may have ten years where they are not well enough to take care of themselves as they did in the past; this will include their ability to manage their own financial affairs. Over time, their ability to keep their home or care for their garden will decline. They may lose their driver's license. Eventually they will lose the energy and interest in their own personal grooming. By being prepared for these eventualities; by working together with your parents, you can put a care plan into place — one that meets with their understanding and their approval.

To give you a visual idea of how the care years might unfold, see Sample 6.

Sample 6
The Care Years Continuum

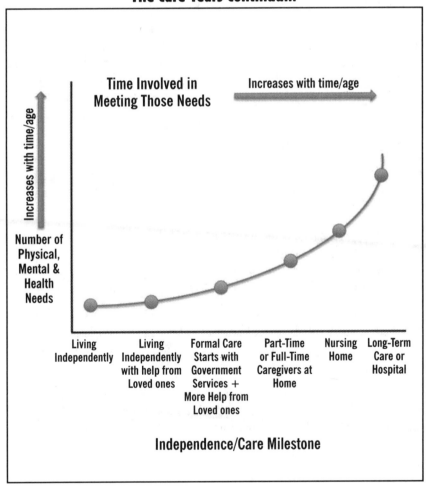

How do you talk to your parents about their wishes for their later years and the financing of those wishes? You may be uncomfortable, and your parents may be reluctant, but it is important to do so while there is still time to put a solid plan in place that reflects their wishes. Waiting too long may mean you will never know what their wishes were and you will be forced to make decisions on your own. If a will, power of attorney (POA), and living will have not been put in place, you may face an uphill battle with family members, your parents' banks and financial advisors, and medical professionals (including doctors, hospitals, and hospices) over your loved one's end-of-life wishes.

It is never too early to have open, direct, and honest conversations with your parents. In the beginning they may not tell you too much. Be prepared for this discussion to take part over many months, or even years. The most important thing is simply to begin.

Begin where it is easiest for you and your family. Each family dynamic includes topics that recur over and over again, be they sports, music, road trips, or family folklore. You might want to ask: "If you could no longer attend baseball games *(insert topic)* because of your arthritis *(insert topic)*, what would you like me to do for you?"

Talk about your memories growing up as a child; share the silly times, the mistakes you made, and how your parents were there for you. These are the times your parents remember best. Their short-term memory may be failing them, but their long-term memories may be intact. Now let them know that you will be there for them when the time comes.

Once your parents are comfortable talking about the past, it is time to talk about the future. The early conversations regarding your parents' wishes should be focused on their goals, lifestyle choices, and health-care options. You may want to ask the following questions:

- If you could not care for yourself, would you want to remain living in your house? For how long?
- If it were no longer safe for you to live at home, what alternatives should we look at?

The more questions you pose, the more you will learn about your parent's wishes. Now, it is most likely you will not be able to "grant" each and every wish, but knowing those wishes will help you to make the choices that most closely reflect them.

Keep in mind that your parents will likely desire to remain in the same community they already live in as it will provide them with continuity in their routines, the comfort of familiar surroundings and the seasons and climate they are used to, and a sense of belonging. They will already have established relationships with medical practitioners in the area, and familiarity with how to access services and the locations. They'll know their local pharmacy, laboratory, hospital, and clinic. If they do not wish to remain in the same community, find out where they want to go and why.

No matter where they end up, they will still need access to healthcare services, shopping, financial services, recreation facilities, a library, religious services, entertainment, restaurants, and a seniors' center. Consider language barriers, festivals, or traditions they enjoy taking part in, and how to be surrounded with people who share similar values and beliefs.

Access to friends and family members will likely be important to them, as it will provide them with physical, social, and psychological support, as well as potential economic supports. Be sure you understand what supports are priorities for your parents.

Consider planning for "driving retirement" as a natural phase of life. While not all older drivers pose a safety hazard, people age 75 and older have more fatal crashes than any other group except teenagers. Drivers who are cognitively impaired (about 25 percent of the 65-and-older group) are seven and a half times more likely as non-impaired drivers to be at fault in a crash, exceeding the rate for drunk drivers.

There are physical and mental changes that happen to all of us as we age, including the following:

- Diminished response time.
- Loss of clarity in vision and hearing.
- Loss of muscle strength and flexibility.
- Reduction in the ability to concentrate.
- Drowsiness due to medications.
- Declining tolerance for alcohol.

Knowing that driving retirement will eventually happen, make sure your parent's plan for where he or she wants to live involves alternatives for getting to the store and to appointments, such as buses, taxis, and friends and family nearby who can drive when needed.

My husband and I have said if we lose our driver's licenses, there will be a reason! We have told our children, the day we lose our driver's licenses is the day they need to begin looking for support services for us, or move us into a retirement home.

Ask if your parents want to live with one of their children or another relative, and, if so, find out if that person is open to having them live with them.

Now it is time to dig a little deeper, and ask about the steps your parents have already taken to achieve their end-of-life wishes. Worksheet 3 will help you work through the important questions to ask your parents (this worksheet is also included in the download kit). If you have siblings, you may want to meet with them and let them know what you are doing and ask if they would like to participate.

2.1 Advantages of having the money talk with your parents

As you will see in the following sections, there are many advantages to having the money talk with your parents.

2.1a To gain clarity

By having open conversations with your parents, you will feel better and have a better sense knowing what is to happen in the future. If there are issues, these can be dealt with before your parents' health declines. Knowing what their wishes are will help you to plan future residences and care.

2.1b To be prepared

Being prepared, having proper powers of attorney in place, and knowing where important documents, online accounts, and PINs are will help you, the caregiver, to step in and make a seamless transition when your parents need help.

From experience, I can tell you that there is no warning when a parent is about to have a heart attack or fall and break a hip. Asking how and where to access information during times of crisis just adds stress on you and your parent at a time when you definitely don't need it.

Worksheet 3
Questions to Ask Your Parents

1. Where do you keep your important papers? Have you prepared a list of all your important papers with relevant contact information? *(Explain that if something were to happen to your parent, knowing where the important papers are will help family to step in and act as quickly and easily as possible in an emergency.)*

2. Do you have a current will? Where do you keep your will? When was the last time it was updated? *(The will should be no more than five years old.)* Who is the executor? Does the person know he or she was chosen to be your executor? *(The will, executors, and beneficiaries should be reviewed after the death of a spouse to ensure your remaining parent's wishes are reflected.)*

3. Have you prepared a power of attorney (POA) document? If no, whom would you like to make decisions for you should you be incapacitated? If yes, whom would you like to appoint for your POA for property and POA for personal care? *(These are two different types of POA so it does not need to be the same person to manage property and personal care.)* Do they know you have chosen them? *(As a concerned family member who is not a POA, you may, with the permission of your parent, want to set up a meeting with the POAs.)*

4. Do you have a safety deposit box? If so, at which bank and where is the key kept?

5. Where are your bank accounts? How many bank accounts do you have? If you were incapacitated, where would I find the PIN and account information? Who has signing authority on your bank accounts?

6. Do you have credit cards? Who are they with? Do you carry a balance or are they paid in full each month?

7. Do you have investments? Who is your financial planner and what is his or her contact information?

8. Who is your accountant and what is his or her contact information?

9. Who is your lawyer and what is his or her contact information?

10. Do you have insurance policies? What company handles the policies? Who is your contact agent?

11. Do you have any debt? Who with? How much do you owe?

12. Do you have any unsettled business? Who, if anyone, owes you money?

2.1c To save money

Significant savings are available to those who plan ahead. American readers can contact the US Department of Housing and Urban Development (HUD), which can help with financial assistance to build or assist with providing supportive housing. Charities and local agencies may have programs to help seniors who need to renovate or repair their homes allowing them to safely stay in their homes longer. Go to SFGate's Home Guides at homeguides.sfgate.com/housing-low-income-seniors-1905.html for more information.

For Canadians, there are government grants available such as money to increase a home's accessibility (visit www.seniors.gc.ca or contact the Canada Mortgage and Housing Corporation for information about the Home Adaptations for Seniors' Independence). Low-income seniors may qualify for what is known as "Rent Geared to Income" accommodation; however, there may be a long waiting list, so early application is very important.

2.1d To get the appropriate level of care for each life stage

In my experience, too many elderly delay moving from the family home. In part, this is because of the long waiting lists to get into appropriate housing, but the biggest reason is that they do not know where to go. No one has done the research or identified the type of housing that is suitable to their life stage or needs. By talking with your parents about their wishes for accommodation, doing the research in advance, and putting their name on a few waiting lists, when the time comes to move, there will be a place to go.

Waiting too long has a financial impact since most people's single largest asset is the family home. Living at home for too long means a delay in liquidating this asset to meet future income needs.

3. Discussing Important Documents with Your Loved One

Of all the choices your parents may make, among the most important will be those they make for their future personal care. To open the conversation, talk to your parents about the importance of making their wishes known while they still can. A loss of capacity either suddenly such as through a stroke, or gradually such as with Alzheimer's, may mean they never have the opportunity to provide their loved ones with their intentions for personal care. This is why it is important to put in place advance directives (AD), powers of attorney (POA) for personal care and for property, and living wills. (**Note:** The names of these forms may vary depending on the jurisdiction in which your parent lives.)

3.1 Power of attorney for personal care

Ensure your parent gives a substitute decision maker the power to act, by completing in writing a power of attorney (POA) for personal care. The substitute decision maker will be called an attorney for personal care (the name may vary depending on where the POA was prepared).

For clarification, the person appointed as a POA does not need to be a lawyer. This term just means that this person was chosen to act on your loved one's behalf. You also don't need to hire a lawyer to draft a power of attorney form, although it is recommended if the person's affairs are complicated. It needs to be properly completed, signed, and witnessed in order to be valid. You can find POA forms on government websites, online, or in bookstores. A lawyer can also help your parent prepare a power of attorney; this may be the best alternative if your parent is having a hard time understanding the information in the POA document.

A POA for personal care is a document through which a substitute decision maker is appointed, giving the person the power to make decisions about *all* aspects of personal care unless otherwise specified. This includes:

- Health
- Shelter
- Clothing
- Nutrition

- Hygiene

- Personal safety

The POA for personal care can only be enacted when the elderly family member is incapable of making his or her own decisions and only as long as he or she is found lacking in that capacity.

It is not uncommon for more than one child to be named as POA for personal care. In my own family, there are three. The reason behind my parents' decision to have three POAs for personal care was to make end-of-life decisions easier, as they thought that giving the responsibility to only one child would cause him or her undue suffering and stress when making life-changing decisions. I may not always agree with the decisions made by my siblings, but luckily for them my displeasure is spread over three people rather than directed at just one of them!

Not appointing a POA for personal care may mean delays in treatment as health-care providers attempt to locate the closest next of kin. If none can be found, the Office of the Public Guardian and Trustee is the substitute decision maker of last resort.

When it comes to carrying out care choices, the substitute decision maker must follow the person's expressed wishes unless it is impossible to do so. For example, many elderly people wish to stay in their own home. The substitute decision maker has a responsibility to honor that wish as long as it is safe to do so and there is community or family support to help ensure that elderly family member's safety.

Consideration must also be given to the financial resources of your elderly family member. Can the person afford to pay for care providers to attend to him or her at home? If so, for how long? It is important to consider that many elderly individuals live longer than might be expected.

3.2 Power of attorney for property

The second type of power of attorney (POA) relates to your parents' finances and property. It is referred to as the power of attorney for property or continuing power of attorney (CPOA). Your parent can choose the same person to be both POA for personal care and POA for property, but he or she can also choose a different person.

Similar to the POA for personal care, the POA for property is a signed, dated, and witnessed legal document that states who the person would like to act on his or her behalf should he or she become mentally incapable. The document must be witnessed and signed by two people in order to be valid. Those witnesses *cannot* be —

- the person's spouse,
- the person's partner,
- the person's children,
- an adult dependent (i.e., a person with an intellectual disability),
- the person's attorney (and not the attorney's spouse or partner),
- anyone younger than the age of majority in the person's jurisdiction, and
- anyone who has a "guardian of property" or "guardian of person" due to his or her own mental incapacity.

Unless your parent restricts the POA's powers, the substitute decision maker will be able to do almost anything that your parent could do concerning his or her finances. The POA can sign documents, start or defend a lawsuit, sell property, make investments, and purchase things for your parent. The POA cannot, however, make a will or prepare a new power of attorney document on your parent's behalf.

In terms of when a POA would come into effect, the person your parent appoints will be able to use the POA as soon as it is signed and witnessed, unless your parent states otherwise within the document itself. Your parent may want to clarify when the POA can come into effect, which could be once he or she has been determined to be incapable of managing his or her own property. If your parent does add this as a clause, it would be wise to say how his or her incapacity should be determined. For example, your parent might require a letter from his or her family doctor. Before your parent sets these types of conditions, know that they may result in complications and delays. Your parent may instead wish to simply have an agreement with an attorney that will be used only if your parent can't look after these matters himself or herself and trust that his or her attorney will make the right decision at the right time.

Your parents can make a POA as long as they, themselves, are mentally capable and know and understand the following:

- what property they have and the value,
- what obligations they have to those who depend on them financially,
- what they are actually giving the POA the authority to do.
- that the POA will be required to account for decisions made about their property,
- that they can revoke or cancel the POA as long as they are mentally capable,
- that if the POA doesn't manage their property well, its value may decrease, and
- that there is always the possibility that the POA could misuse his or her authority.

Anyone older than the age of majority can be appointed as a POA. More than one person can be appointed as POA. The POA is not the same as the executor in a will. Those two positions are not related in any way, although your parent can certainly choose the same person to act as both.

Choosing a POA is extremely important, as this person will have full access to your parent's money and other property. When you're helping your parent choose a POA, the following are some key factors he or she should consider in making the decision:

- Is the person willing to take on the POA role and its responsibilities?
- Will the person be able to live up to the high standards set out by the law for this role?
- Is the person trustworthy, responsible, and good at handling money?
- Will the person help make sure your parent has everything and anything he or she needs?
- Will the person respect your parent's privacy?

Many people find the process of choosing a POA stressful because they worry it will cause conflict with other family members and loved ones. Conflict can often be avoided simply by having your parent inform everybody of his or her choice in advance, and any reasons he or she had for choosing that person. One common reason for conflict is that the majority of your family will not know what the POA is doing with the money, but this can easily be avoided by appointing more than one person as POA and requiring that both people approve all decisions and transactions.

The family I introduced you to in Chapter 1 — Grace, and her daughters Linda and Mary — encountered many frustrations and emotional challenges throughout this process. Knowing Grace as I do, she set up her affairs with the best of intentions, based on her knowledge of who had the best track record of being fiscally responsible, and who would be best at confronting the harsh realities of when her ability to care for herself was suffering. In my opinion, she made the right choices, but I know it has caused friction for her two lovely daughters.

When times are stressful, such as when a family is dealing with a parent's illness, siblings can often act out their anxiety, anger, and grief on each other. Some siblings set up in "camp denial" where they do not want to accept what is happening to their parent. Some react like lions, with rage and anger, and take it out on other family members. Others act like rabbits, staying out of the fray, voicing no emotions, and making themselves scarce. While all siblings love their parents and want what is best for them, the range and expressions of those emotions can be wildly different for each person.

Grace's daughter Linda, who was named the sole POA for property and the joint POA for personal care (along with Mary), found it "devastating" (in Linda's words) to have the POA put in place because it meant deeming her mother incompetent. She was very overwhelmed by the process since there was so much to learn, and found it especially challenging to deal with at the same time they were all learning about Grace's Alzheimer's diagnosis. Dealing with her mom's lawyer felt frustrating too, as Linda was used to working with her mom as a team. During this process the responsibility the lawyer had was to act purely in her mother's interest, which felt to Linda as if the lawyer was protecting her mother *from* her.

Mary, who was named a joint POA for personal care along with Linda, felt very out of the loop and somewhat bitter (a common and understandable emotion) that she was to be excluded from anything to do with her mother's finances, but through her journey to become informed, she eventually realized that she could still ask her sister for a report on how her mother's funds are being managed on an annual basis.

While they both have their mother's best interests at heart, it is still a test of their sibling relationship. It is difficult for them to have to live with the decisions their mother made in terms of the POA arrangement, especially when it is difficult to ask her to articulate her reasons now that she is dealing with Alzheimer's.

Make sure the power of attorney (POA) documents are kept somewhere safe that will be accessible many years in the future, even if people move, pass away, or forget. Many people keep a copy on file with their lawyer. I also recommend that the POA or elderly parent goes to the financial institutions and banks your parents are working with and ask them to keep a copy of the POA for property documents in their files. Ask for confirmation that they are on file. You should also send a copy to any other financial institutions with which your parent deals. The financial institutions should be willing to keep a copy on file at the request of the client (elderly parent in this case). The banks and financial institutions will still require proof the POA has been enacted before taking direction from the named POA.

3.2a Tips for making decisions as a power of attorney

Acting as a power of attorney (POA) can be stressful. Making decisions for someone you love without being able to get his or her input can be overwhelming and cause you to second-guess yourself. Here are a few guidelines to help you act ethically and responsibly:

- Stop and think before you act. Sometimes taking a bit of time — unless it is an emergency — can prevent rash decisions and help you come to more thoughtful answers. Even in an emergency, take a few deep breaths before you make a decision.

- Keep goals in mind. Try to balance the "now" with the "later" so that by choosing something with short-term needs in mind you won't compromise long-term goals.

- Get the facts. Take the time to get all the information you need before you make a decision. Talk to professionals when needed.

- Consider all options.

- Consider all consequences. Will the consequences of any options violate any of your core values and principles, such as trustworthiness, respect, responsibility, fairness, caring, or citizenship? If so, eliminate those options. You can never go wrong with the Golden Rule: Do unto others as you would have them do unto you.

- Make the choice.

- Monitor and modify as needed. Make sure the choice you made is getting the results you expected. If not, make modifications.

3.2b What you can do when you're not appointed power of attorney

If you, like Mary, are not appointed power of attorney (POA) and you are concerned, there are still things you can do. If the POA is someone other than yourself, you may be wondering how to work with the POA as well as the details of your rights and limitations.

The first thing to remember is that your parents, in their wisdom, have purposefully chosen someone else to act as their substitute decision maker. The second is that you have my complete understanding, as I have found myself in a similar situation. In my case, I had to remind myself that my parents were very simple people, who were now very elderly. My father lived to age 95, my mother is still living at age 89, and their understanding of who I am and my professional credentials have not kept up with their image of me as a young girl.

During the two very difficult years leading up to my father's death, I learned what I could do to help the POA he chose:

- Offer to help the POAs for personal care and property. If the POAs are your remaining healthy parent or siblings, they are facing the same emotional turmoil you are. They may be overwhelmed with their roles, and the amount of work required to properly care for your parent. They too, love your parent and want what is best for him or her (if you believe this is not the case, see the last point in this section).

- Send a copy of this book to the POAs with a letter, letting them know you have found it to be a helpful tool.

- Offer to take on some of the non-POA tasks such as taking your elderly parent shopping, taking him or her to the hairdresser, or simply taking him or her out for a nice lunch.

- If you enjoy searching the Internet, you may want to offer to research the appropriate and available programs or care facilities for your parents. Providing the POAs with a short list for them to review and select from would undoubtedly be very helpful. Many of the tools found in this book can be used to assist you in preparing a checklist or comparison.

- Don't be shy. Be respectful, but not shy in bringing your concerns about your parent's diminishing capacity to the attention of the POAs. No food in your parent's house? Fear your parent is not receiving or taking the proper medications? You have an obligation to let the POAs know.

- POAs who are not responding quickly enough may be a concern for you. In my family, the lead POA seemed to be in a state of perpetual denial. Denial may be a protective measure for the person who is experiencing it, but it can be very dangerous for your elderly parents who may not receive the care they need when they need it.

    What can you do? Write to your parent's family doctor. Introduce yourself and tell him or her that you are not the POA and your letter is to alert the doctor that there may be some health and capacity issues. Ask the doctor to help you by scheduling an appointment with your parent and the POA(s) for personal care. Provide the doctor with the name and contact information of the POAs. In my own experience, this worked very well. The doctor called my mother within a week to book an appointment for a complete medical assessment. The doctor suggested it was time for mom to move so she would have supervised care.

- Call your local community care access center for seniors. They can, and will, accept calls of concern from any interested party. They will make arrangements for various assessments to ensure your parent is safe. In my experience, they were helpful when I could not convince the POAs or other family members of my legitimate concerns.

- If your elderly parent has landed in the hospital emergency room, and the hospital staff has let your family know they will be keeping him or her for a period of time (e.g., 72 hours) before discharge, take note that this is a warning that the hospital staff may have concerns about returning your parent to his or her home.

    If the hospital staff calls a family meeting, this is large red flag! *Please* attend the meeting and make your concerns known. You and the input you can provide are the very reason they are calling the meeting. The staff is worried about your parent.

- In situations where your elderly parent is being taken advantage of or abused (whether there is a POA or not), as a concerned family member, you can seek help from your state or provincial guardianship department. The government authority may be brought in to act as your parent's guardian. Though they may not know your parent's every wish, they are bound to act in your parent's best interest, including placement in facility care when necessary. Their mandate is not to protect any possible inheritance, but rather to ensure your parent receives the quality care he or she needs. If you're still not sure how to proceed, seek legal advice. A lawyer can help you to apply for guardianship of your parent or help you with the application to the government for guardianship.

If you have concerns about mismanagement of funds or theft, your parent (if he or she is mentally capable) may elect to revoke (cancel) the power of attorney, demand a full accounting, and consider making a claim for any lost funds. If the matter involves theft, a report to the police should be considered. The court may be asked to review the accounts and records the POA is required to keep. This process is called a "passing of accounts." You may also wish to report the matter to the Office of the Public Guardian and Trustee (depending on your jurisdiction, the government office name may be different). They investigate allegations involving a mentally incapable person who is believed to be at serious financial risk.

To help minimize the potential for POAs abusing their power, many in the legal and financial profession recommend that clients do one or more of the following:

- Name more than one person as the POA (that way no one person can act opportunistically without accountability).

- Include a clause that the POAs must submit periodic financial statements to the client's accountant, lawyer, or other trusted individual who can monitor how money is being used.

- Limit the ability of the POA to make gifts or changes to interest in the client's property.

- Choose someone other than the POA to activate the POA document and ask for a capacity assessment. The client should specify two doctors (whom he or she has chosen) to evaluate his or her mental capacity.

3.3 Will

When it comes to your parents' wills, you need to find out where they are located, if they are current, and whether or not the wills reflect their wishes accurately.

Wills should be reviewed every five years or whenever the family dynamic changes to ensure they accurately reflect your parents' wishes. Changes that require review would include the following:

- Births or adoptions
- Marriage or divorce
- A family member becoming disabled
- A family member becoming a spendthrift
- Someone getting in trouble with the law

Your parent may have very strong feelings about bequeathing an inheritance so his or her wishes need to be reflected in his or her will. While you can help your parent by booking an appointment with a qualified estate lawyer to update a will, please be respectful once your parent and the lawyer meet, as the lawyer's client is your parent, not you. The lawyer's job is to draw up a will that is in keeping with your parent's wishes.

3.4 Living will

A living will is sometimes called an advance-care directive. It is not the same as a POA for personal care. This document is used to express the wishes of your elderly family member about the care he or she wants to receive and is most often related to end-of-life care. It informs loved ones of the person's wishes for such things as extreme measures to keep him or her alive or when to remove life support. It may address the issue of forced feeding or the use of narcotics to keep the person free from pain. It too can only be used when the person can no longer make decisions for himself or herself. The following are some of the questions a living will may answer:

- When is it prudent to undergo invasive surgery?
- When is it time to pull the plug on life-extending procedures?
- When it is time to begin medications to ease the pain at end of life?
- When it is time to move to palliative care or hospice?

3.5 Advance directive

An Advance Directive (AD) is a statement of the person's wishes made while he or she is still capable. Completing an AD gives your parent control over his or her future care options and wishes. It makes wishes known and gives someone the person trusts the authority to act on those wishes, if the need arises. The person selected to act on your parents' behalf is called the "substitute decision maker" (the name may vary depending on where the person lives).

When creating an AD, your parents may express their wishes about anything related to their personal care, for instance:

- Where they want to live.
- What they want to eat.
- What they want to wear.
- What level of grooming they desire.
- The kind of health care they want.
- The steps they want you to take to ensure they are safe.

Who decides if a person is no longer capable of making decisions? The health-care provider offering treatment decides whether your elderly family member has the capacity or not to make decisions about his or her treatment, admission to a long-term care home, or personal assistance services. This kind of assessment is ongoing rather than a one-time event because the ability to make decisions in one area of life may not be impacted in another, or the ability to make decisions may vary based on the person's health condition at the time and could change from month to month or even weekly.

Should they become incapacitated and incapable of making decisions on their own, the AD should be taken to your parents' health-care providers who will then be required to take direction from the substitute decision maker. Gather all of the relevant information from various health-care providers about past medical care, treatment, and medications.

The substitute decision maker, wherever possible, must follow the wishes of the elderly family member. When this is not possible, the person has a responsibility to place the safety and welfare of his or her elderly family member first. As the substitute decision maker, you are responsible for maintaining contact and involving the elderly family member as much as possible in any decisions regarding his or her care.

Follow the care wishes as much as possible. Note that it is not possible to lay out in advance all possible scenarios. Simply try to consider the best alternatives based on your knowledge of your elderly parents' values and beliefs. Weigh the possible benefits and risks of any course of action, and make decisions based on what you believe to be in your parents' best interests.

4. The Five Wishes

Five Wishes is a tool for developing an advance directive document, including the living will, and was developed in the United States. It talks about the person's emotional needs, medical wishes, and spiritual needs. Developed in part by the American Bar Association to help people deal with the legal problems in end-of-life care, this model can also be used informally in Canada as a starting point for discussion.

If you are working with your elderly parents, choose a quiet moment to introduce a conversation about the five wishes concept. You may be surprised by their answers. It is a good idea to document the answers. American readers can formalize the five wishes as part of their legal documents. Canadian readers may add a signed and dated letter outlining their five wishes to their POA and will documents.

Five Wishes allows a person to spell out exactly how he or she wants to be treated should he or she become seriously ill. Note that specific funeral instructions, memorial services, and burial requests may be included in this document. Give your parent time to think about the following questions in Worksheet 4 (a variation of this form is included in the download kit).

5. Organize

One of the most comprehensive online tools I have found for collecting and organizing personal records is from the Canadian Life and Health Insurance Association Inc. (bit.ly/personalrecords; accessed January 20, 2014). You'll find "Your Virtual Shoebox Guide" extremely helpful in identifying the many account numbers, passwords, and personal and financial information you'll need as you work through the processes in this book with your parents. Whether you keep it as an online file, or as a hard copy in a binder, it can be your go-to document whenever you have to provide information to a

Worksheet 4
Five Wishes

Wish 1: **Who do you wish to make health-care decisions for you when you can't make them for yourself?**

Choose someone who knows you very well, cares about you, and who is able to make difficult decisions. Family members or your spouse may not be the best choice as they are too emotionally involved. Choose someone who is able to stand up for your wishes and lives close enough to help whenever needed.

Be sure to discuss your wishes with this person; first ask if he or she is willing and able to take on this responsibility. You will need to fully discuss your wishes with this person. Ask if he or she is prepared to act on your wishes.

Wish 2: **What is your wish for the type of medical treatment you want?**

Traditionally this wish begins with the following statement:

I believe that my life is precious and I deserve to be treated with dignity. When the time comes that I am very sick and I am not able to speak for myself, I want the following wishes and any other directions I have given to my health-care agent, to be respected and followed.

Describe your wishes for pain management, comfort issues, life support or extraordinary measures and what to do in specific situations (e.g., close to death, in a coma, or having permanent and severe brain injury with no expectation of recovery).

Wish 3: **How comfortable do you wish to be?**

This wish may contain specific requests; for example, music to be played, poems or favorite passages read out loud, or photos to be kept nearby.

This may include information about your grooming needs and cleanliness of bed and towel linens.

Wish 4: How do you wish people will treat you?

This wish may include requests for who you want by your side in your dying days such as whom you would like to see (e.g., family, friends, clergy) and whether or not you want someone by your side to comfort you. You can also specify that you want to die in your own home (if possible) or to be in a facility with professional caregivers while family and friends visit as guests (as opposed to being caregivers).

Wish 5: What do you wish your loved ones to know?

This wish may contain statements that you want the family to know; for example, that you love them, or you may ask for forgiveness for times you have hurt family, friends, or others. It may also show forgiveness for hurts you have experienced from others. It is a wish that can evoke a need to make peace with yourself, your family, and your community; or to remind loved ones to celebrate your life with memories of joy, not sorrow.

third party (e.g., financial advisor, doctor, lawyer) or when you need to share information with other family members.

Now that you have learned about how to have the important conversations with your parents regarding their future wishes for care and accommodation, and you have helped them decide on who will be responsible for executing those wishes (the POAs), and you know how and when to step in if necessary, it's time to think about helping them create a financial plan that will secure the funds needed to make all those wishes happen.

chapter 4

A Financial Plan for Your Parents

Once you have your own plan for retirement in place, and you've had discussions with your parents about what their needs and wants will be as they age, it's time to put together a solid financial plan for them.

When I reflect on Grace's situation, I remember that after that first meeting with her and her two daughters, my next meeting with her was to complete a review of her financial plan. We did an updated net worth statement, a detailed review of investment assets, and a review of the current portfolio asset allocations, and compared them to the target as stated in the investment policy statement, and we looked at her rate of return since our last review. We then looked at any income that had been taken from the assets and how much capital had been drawn down, so we could compare it to our target and ensure Grace's lifestyle was going to be sustainable. This was also a great time to answer any questions that Grace and her daughters had (they had many).

The following steps are from the Canadian Financial Planner guidelines (www.fpsc.ca/financial-planning-process, accessed January 29, 2014):

- **Step 1:** Create a financial plan to establish goals. If you have already had the conversations recommended in Chapter 3, then you should have a clear idea of your parents' wishes and goals.

- **Step 2:** Gather all relevant information regarding your parents' assets, liabilities, sources of income and timing of those income payments, and expenses, and assembling all of this information into an organized binder or file (as you do this, you may want to revisit the Seven-Step Action Plan for Caregivers in Chapter 1). Once you have done that, you are ready to create a net worth statement and a cash flow statement of your parents' affairs. Having clarity about your parents' financial situation, you will be in a position to help your parents.

- **Step 3:** Review possible strategies.

- **Step 4:** Create an action plan to optimize your parents' situation.

- **Step 5:** Monitor, review, and update concerned parties as well as the financial planner you're working with on a regular basis and as circumstances change.

Let's get into the process in more detail so that you know exactly what to do and how to do it.

1. Step 1: Establish Goals

Review the conversations you had with your parents in Chapter 3. Make sure that you understand exactly what they want to achieve through their remaining years, and the funds that will be required at each stage. Once it is all on paper, through powers of attorney, wills, and additional notes that you may have taken throughout the process, you're ready to build a plan to make it all happen.

2. Step 2: Gather Information

Collecting all the pertinent information to fully understand your parents' financial situation can seem daunting at first. You may not know where they keep their paperwork, and they, like many others, may not have organized all their papers in the most user-friendly or easy-to-find manner. Don't get frustrated. You will find everything you need, even if it takes some time.

Worksheet 5 will help you prepare for the net worth, and cash flow statements in this chapter. If you are working with a financial planner, he or she will be able to use this information to build a financial plan for your parents. This list is very comprehensive, so keep in mind that not all types of documents will be applicable, as they depend on your parents' age and working status.

2.1 Net worth statement

The next thing you'll need to do is complete a net worth statement for your parents. This is a financial statement that will list your parent's assets and liabilities and their values as of a specific date. Ultimately, when you look at the excess of total assets over total liabilities, you are left with an amount known as "net worth." (See Sample 7.) So that you can help your parents prepare their own net worth statements, you'll find the editable Net Worth Statement in MS Excel format in the download kit.

It is helpful to track these amounts from year to year, in one spreadsheet, so that you can see any growth or decline in the amounts contained therein. In the download kit, you'll find a Multi-Year Net Worth Tracker.

2.2 Cash flow statement

The next part of the process of gathering all of your parents' relevant information is to create a cash flow statement so you can see where their money is going. It is an essential part of budgeting and gathering information before you make a financial plan. See Sample 8.

In the download kit you will find a Cash Flow Statement so you can help your parents organize their incoming and outgoing cash flow. **Note:** When entering amounts related to income in the form, always use pretax amounts. Tax will be deducted on a separate line within the template.

2.3 Budgeting

A big part of making a plan for your parents is budgeting. The US Department of Health & Human Services reports in its "A Profile of Older Americans" brochure[1], in 2011 the median income for those aged 65 and older was $25,704 for males and $15,075 for females with couples earning $45,763. Only 53 percent of American seniors

---

1 "A Profile of Older Americans: 2011," US Department of Health and Human Services Administration on Aging, accessed January 20, 2014.
www.aoa.gov/Aging_Statistics/Profile/2011/docs/2011profile.pdf.

Worksheet 5
Financial Planning Preparation

Type of Document	What You Need to Find
All individual and registered retirement accounts (i.e., 401(k), RRSP, RIF, LIRA, and LIF)	Copies of the most recent statements, which show the financial institution involved, type of investment, contributions, and current values.
Roth Individual Retirement Account (IRA) or Tax-Free Savings Account (TFSA)	Copies of the most recent statements, which show the financial institution involved, type of investment, contributions, and current values.
Other Investments	For any non-registered investments find copies of the most recent statements and ensure they show the financial institution involved, type of investment, contributions, and current values. Ask for an asset allocation model of the current investments and rate of return for the past three to five years. Include Guaranteed Investment Certificate (GIC) statements. As for annuities, get the income details and number of remaining payments.
Pension Plan	Copies of the pension plan details and the most recent pension plan statement showing current values and retirement income. If you cannot find one, contact the human resources department of your parent's former employer for assistance. Don't forget to ask about survivor benefits.
Bank Statements	Copies of all bank account statements including checking and saving accounts. Some people keep multiple bank accounts earmarked for a variety of purposes.

Tax Returns	A copy of the most recent tax returns for the past two years.
RRSP Carry Forward Amounts (Canadian)	If your parent is younger than the age of 71, find the most recent "Notice of Assessment" from the Canada Revenue Agency (CRA), which will show the tax credits received and the remaining contribution room to a Registered Retirement Savings Plan.
539 Plans and Registered Education Savings Plan (RESP) Statements	A copy of the most recent statements, showing the financial institution, type of investment, contributions, and current values.
Group Benefits	A copy of the most recent booklet detailing amounts of life insurance, disability, or critical illness benefits, health and dental benefits, from your parent's past employer.
Disability Insurance Policies	A copy of any disability insurance policies.
Critical Illness Insurance Policies	A copy of any critical illness insurance policies.
Life Insurance	A copy of any personal and corporate policies on your parent's life and/or family members.
Wills	A copy of the most recent will for each parent.
Powers of Attorney	A copy of the most recent powers of attorney.
Income	A detailed list of government benefits (e.g., Social Security, Social Assistance, CPP, OAS, pension, and GIS). If your parent is still working, you'll need a list of salary, commissions and fees, and bonuses for the current year.

Mortgage Statements	A copy of the most recent statements for principal residences, recreational property, and investment properties. You need to be sure the statements show the financial institution involved, terms of the mortgage (i.e., interest rate, years of amortization), payment options, and current balances.
Liabilities	A detailed listing of any liabilities (e.g., bank loans, vehicle loans, credit card balances, loans to family or friends).
Current Financial Plan	If one exists, collect a copy of the most recent financial plan.
Advisors • Lawyer • Accountant • Insurance agent • Financial advisor • Family doctor • Dentist • Other specialist • Pharmacist	Collect the name, address, and telephone number for your parent's advisors and medical providers.
Business Interests and Ownership Details	Find out the current estimated fair market value, share structure, and liabilities. You'll also want copies of the buy and sell agreement and current financial statements.

Sample 7
Net Worth Statement

Net Worth Statement							
Assets	**Husband**	**Wife**	**Combined**	**Liabilities**	**Husband**	**Wife**	**Combined**
Real Estate				**Mortgage**			
Family Home	$ 200,000.00	$ 200,000.00	$ 400,000.00	Family Home			
Cottage/Second Home	$ 75,000.00		$ 75,000.00	Cottage	$ 60,000.00		$ 60,000.00
				Vehicle Loan	15,000.00	$ 7,500.00	22,500.00
Investments				**Credit Card Balances**			
Non-Registered Investments	60,000.00	60,000.00	120,000.00	card 1		600.00	600.00
401(k) RRSP	30,000.00	50,000.00	80,000.00	card 2			
LIRA/LIF	175,000.00		175,000.00	card 3			
Roth IRA/TESA	35,000.00	35,000.00	70,000.00				
529 Plan/RESP	15,000.00	50,000.00	65,000.00				
Cash	7,500.00	7,500.00	15,000.00				
Other							
Vehicles	35,000.00	15,000.00	50,000.00				
Collectibles							
Other							
Inheritance		27,500.00	27,500.00				
SUBTOTAL	$ 632,500.00	$ 445,000.00	$ 1,077,500.00	**SUBTOTAL**	$ 75,000.00	$ 8,100.00	$ 83,100.00
Total							$ 994,400.00

Cash Flow Statement

Cash Flow Statement

	Spouse 1	Spouse 2	Joint
Cash Inflows: Monthly			
Investment Income			
Non-Registered Investments			
Interest	$156	$100	$256
Dividends	200	200	400
Capital Gains	72		72
Prescribed Life Annuity:			
Taxable Portion		150	150
Return of Capital:			
Non Taxable (all sources)	100	1,000	1,100
Pension Income			
Social Assistance/OAS	546	546	1,092
Social Security/CPP/QPP	1,012	528	1,540
401(k)/RRSP			
RRIF/LIF		225	225
Defined Benefit Pension	670		670
Disability Benefit			
Veterans Affairs	175		175
Total Cash Inflows	**$2,931**	**$2,749**	**$5,680**
TOTAL INCOME FROM ALL SOURCES			

Expenses: Monthly		**Expenses: Monthly**	
Food	380	**Financial Obligations**	
Housing		**Savings**	
Mortgage/Rent	900	Contributions	
Utilities (e.g., heat, electricity)	250	Roth IRA/TFSA	300
Phone/Cell/Internet	87	Loan Payments	100
Home Insurance	90	Credit Card Payments	75
Property Tax	250	**Insurance Premiums**	
Condominuim Fees		Life Insurance	67
Maintenance	100	Disability Insurance	
Housekeeping	80	Critical Illness	
Lawn/Snow Removal	75	Long-Term Care	350
Transportation		Health Insurance	125
Gas/Fuel	100	Travel Insurance	15
Car Insurance	75	**Recreation/Leisure**	
Loan/Lease Payment	251	Fitness/Club Membership	25
Maintenance/Repairs	65	Travel/Vacation	250
Parking	10	Hobbies	35
Public Tranportation	25	Pets	
Daily Living		Entertainment	125
Clothing	125	Subscriptions	15
Grooming/Personal Care	75	Tobacco/Alcohol	60
Health Care		**Miscellaneous**	
Eye/Dental	35	Gifts	100
Prescription	12	Charities	100
Home Care	100	Other	
Respite	50	**Income Taxes**	565
Other			
Subtotal	**$3,135**		**$2,307**
Total Cash Inflows			**$5,442**

reported income from assets (i.e., investments). According to Statistics Canada (in 2011), the average before-tax income for a retired couple (older than age 65) was $63,800.[2] That number drops to $32,800 for a single elderly female. Budgeting thoughtfully will help make the most of every dollar and ensure your parents are living within their means in a way that is sustainable.

There is a big cost involved with our parents' generation (as there will be to those who follow) thanks to how much longer we are now living. Prices for long-term care are on the rise. The average cost of a retirement home or long-term care facility can range from $3,000 to $6,000 per month. Those costs do not include medication management, or assistance with dressing or bathing. Total costs can escalate up to $10,000 per month for premium care in a luxury facility. You need to compare facility costs with those associated with your parent staying at home. While it may seem far more expensive to be in a facility, keep in mind that those costs include utilities and meals. Staying at home costs mean additional fees of phone bills, hydro bills, groceries, lawn care, snow shoveling, repairs and maintenance, and more.

Budgeting also needs to take into account that your parents may face some unexpected or extraordinary expenses. These may include a new roof for the house or replacing a furnace, or other replacement and upkeep costs that don't happen on a monthly or annual basis. Other things to consider include home renovations that would be necessary to help them live independently for a longer period of time (e.g., wheelchair ramp, walk-in bathtub, an elevator to get upstairs).

If your parents are still in good health and living independently, this is the time to revisit the Five Retirement Lifestyle Budgets (discussed in Chapter 2) and figure out which one applies to your parents so you can budget according to their financial plan. How do they spend their time and money? Even if you haven't given it much thought, you probably already have a good idea of what your elderly family members enjoy about their retirement.

Is it slower-paced days with time to do whatever they want? Maybe they enjoy reading a good book under the shade of an old oak tree. Maybe something more active is their cup of tea, such as socializing with friends and family, or playing with great grandchildren. Do they own a retirement home, or travel? You will need to budget for the cost of increasing health and medical care too.

---

2 www.statcan.gc.ca/tables-tableaux/sum-som/l01/cst01/famil05a-eng.htm, accessed January 20, 2014.

2.4 Look at your parents' investments

Now it's time to look at any investments your parents have. What is the size of their portfolio? How much are they drawing down (i.e., withdrawing, using, spending) on a monthly and annual basis? Are they drawing down more or less than the portfolio rate of return? As your parents age, it is not unusual for them to draw down more income than the portfolio rate of return, but it is important to consider whether they are living beyond their means. Alternatively, they may be acting overly frugal, as is common for people who lived through the Great Depression of the 1930s.

Look at how many years they may be expected to live, and calculate whether that draw-down amount is sustainable for that long. Err on the side of caution and add five years to their estimated longevity.

These types of calculations are often best done with the help of your parents' financial planner. If they do not have one, it is a good idea to begin partnering with one at this time.

When you are thinking of your parents' home as part of their assets, and as a potential source of income, I always suggest seeing the home as the asset of last resort. When I work with clients, I call their home their "health and welfare account" since the sale of the home can free up cash that can be used to fund their later years in a retirement home or facility, and contribute to medical expenses.

Chapter 7 will review investment strategies for your elderly parents.

3. Step 3: Review Possible Strategies

Once you have completed the net worth and cash flow statements, you will have a good idea of your parents' current financial situation. Take some time to review the information you have collected. Do you see any obvious areas for improvement? Are your parents in good financial shape? Do you see a problem now, or coming in the future?

Worksheet 6 lists a few items to review with your parents. I would urge you to *consider each point, investigate* how applicable it is to your parents' situation, and *act* on the items which need changing.

There may be even more you can do to maximize their income or minimize expenditures through tax strategies, which will be covered in more detail in Chapter 5.

4. Step 4: Create the Action Plan

Once you have reviewed the suggested strategies in Worksheet 6, create an action plan. Keep reading, as you will find many more useful strategies in this book to help you create your action plan. Topics will include investment and tax strategies, when to move to facility care, how to sell the family home, and tips for reducing the stress of moving your parents to a retirement home or care facility.

If all of this seems overwhelming, especially at a time where you are worried about your parents' well-being, hire a qualified financial planner to help you. Look for an advisor who also holds their Certified Professional Consultant on Aging (CPCA) designation. Advisors who have the CPCA designation have demonstrated an interest in, and ability to work with, the elderly. In Chapter 11 you will find some helpful tips for hiring a team of professionals.

5. Step 5: Monitor, Review, and Update the Action Plan Regularly

Once you put the plan into action, it will be necessary to monitor all the financial elements on a regular basis. Your parents (or you, or their power of attorney) will need to track their expenses to ensure they are in line with expectations, and keep track of their investments (e.g., watch for changes that may result from market fluctuations or changing interest rates). Extraordinary expenses that crop up will also need to be factored in when and if they arise, causing possible reevaluation of the plan to accommodate those expenses.

Reporting to your parents, their accountant, and other siblings (with your parent's permission) may be necessary and advisable so that everyone feels kept in the loop.

If you or your siblings need to spend money out-of-pocket on your parent's behalf, you may find Worksheet 7 handy for tracking expenses and reimbursement. (You will find an Out-of-Pocket Expense Tracker in the download kit.)

Worksheet 6
Reviewing Documents: Consider, Investigate, and Act

Type of Document	Consider—Investigate—Act
All Registered Retirement Accounts (e.g., 401(k), RRSP, RIF, LIRA, and LIF)	• How much income do your parents draw from their registered accounts? • Do they draw the minimum required or more? (Drawing more than the minimum may mean they are paying more taxes than need be.)
Roth Individual Retirement Account (IRA) or Tax-Free Savings Account (TFSA)	• If your parents have a cash surplus each year, are they contributing to Roth IRAs or TFSAs? (This is a good place to build an emergency fund.)
Other Investments	• Are your parents' non-registered investments tax efficient? • Would rebalancing of their portfolio allow them to reduce taxation? • If your parents are Canadian, are they subject to an Old Age Security (OAS) clawback?
Pension Plan	• Review the pension plan document. • Will your parents' income change over time? • How long does the income continue? • Is the income indexed to inflation? • At the time of death of the pensioner, how much will his or her spouse receive?
Bank Statements	• Too many bank accounts? (Consider consolidating to two accounts; one for paying all regular fixed costs and a second account to use when paying for grooming, shopping, recreation, and food.)
Tax Returns	• Talk to your parents' tax planner and ask if they are taking full advantage of the tax breaks available to them.
RRSP Carry Forward Amounts (Canadian)	• If your parents are younger than the age of 71, and they are working either part- or full-time, can they make RRSP contributions? • How much would they save in taxation by making this RRSP contribution?

539 Plans and Registered Education Savings Plan (RESP) Statements	• Many grandparents enjoy providing their grandchildren with a lasting gift. Assuming your parents can afford to, do they have an interest in opening this type of account for their grandchildren?
Group Benefits	• If your parents are still working, are they taking full advantage of their group benefits? • Some retirees from the corporate world continue to receive health and dental benefits from a former employer. • Are your parents participating in the retiree group plans available to them?
Disability Insurance Policies	• Has your parent suffered from a disability while covered by disability insurance? • Has he or she made a claim? • If your parent was wounded in active service, has he or she made a claim to Veterans Affairs (Canada)? • Does he or she continue to pay premiums on a policy where he or she is no longer eligible to collect a benefit? (Most disability policies do not pay benefits to retirees.) • Book an appointment with the agent to review.
Critical Illness Insurance Policies	• If your parent has critical illness insurance, either through an employer or personal coverage—and has a listed critical illness— has he or she made a claim?
Long-Term Care Insurance Policies	• Do your parents own a long-term care insurance policy? (If they do not own a policy, you may wish to investigate their eligibility.) • Can they still perform the activities of daily living? • Call your parents' insurance agent to review.
Life Insurance	• Do your parents have adequate life insurance coverage? • Do they have older policies with cash values? (Older policies have many uses, and can even offer cash benefits to the living.)

	• When was the last time these were reviewed by their life insurance agent? (Many older policies can be put on premium vacation, which is a break from paying premiums.) • Are the beneficiaries still alive? Is there a need for change? • Do your parents wish to leave a charitable bequest or gift? • Book an appointment with the agent to review.
Wills	• Are their wills up to date and do they reflect their wishes?
Powers of Attorney	• Are the powers of attorney documents (i.e., personal care and property) up to date?
Income	• Review all income sources. • Are your parents receiving all of the government benefits available to them? • Has your widowed parent applied for a widow's benefit? • How will the death of one spouse impact the future income of the survivor? • Are your parents receiving income in the most tax-efficient manner? • If they live in Canada, do they qualify for a Guaranteed Income Supplement (GIS)? Has an application been made?
Mortgage Statements	• If your parents have a debt and non-registered savings, have they considered reducing or eliminating their debt? • What are the prepayment terms of their mortgage? • How quickly can they pay down the mortgage without penalty? • When is the mortgage renewal date? • Can the mortgage be refinanced at a lower rate?

Liabilities	• For bank loans, vehicle loans, and credit card balances, consider consolidating high interest debt for a lower cost personal line of credit. • For loans to family or friends, perhaps it is time to collect?
Current Financial Plan	• Is it up to date? • When was the last time it was updated? (Financial plans should be updated every few years or as circumstances change.)
Advisors • Lawyer • Accountant • Insurance Agent • Financial Advisor • Family Doctor • Dentist • Other Specialist • Pharmacist	• Have you contacted your parents' advisors to introduce yourself? • Have you provided your parents' advisors with a copy of the powers of attorney? • Have you booked a meeting to familiarize yourself with your parents' affairs and your responsibilities? • Concerned about your parents' medications? (Ask the pharmacist to prepackage each day's medication in blister packs, delivered one week at a time.)
Business Interests and Ownership Details	• Contact the tax and legal advisors for your parent. Introduce yourself and submit notarized copies of the power of attorney for property. • The lawyer should have the most recent buy and sell agreements and share ownership documents. • The accountant will have an understanding of value and may provide direction in seeking an appraisal. • Hire a business appraiser. • Meet with a qualified Certified Financial Planner who has experience working with business owners, as the rules can change frequently and the complexity requires a high level of knowledge.

Worksheet 7
Out-of-Pocket Expense Tracker

Out-of-Pocket Expense Tracker							
Date of Purchase	Person Who Bought Item	Item Purchased	Where	Amount Owed (attach receipt)	Date Reimbursed	Amount Reimbursed	Check Number
01/15/14	Lise	Advil	Walgreens	$7.49	01/18/14	$7.49	#0001
Monthly Total				**$7.49**		**$7.49**	

chapter 5

Maximizing Every Dollar

According to Statistics Canada, in 2011 more than 11 percent of Canadians aged 65 and older were considered to be in the "low income before tax" category[1]. The Government of Canada defines a set of income cutoffs below which a person would be considered to live in straitened (financially limited) circumstances, also known as "low income." As per the Government of Canada's website, this is generally when a person has to spend significantly more than 50 percent of his or her income on food, clothing, and shelter. For example, if an individual (or those tied together in one economic household) had to spend 70 percent on those three expenses alone, that would not likely leave enough for transportation, health care, personal care, education, household operation, recreation, and insurance.

American readers should take note that in 2010, 3.5 million (9 percent) of elderly persons lived below the poverty line. This number

---

1 www.statcan.gc.ca/tables-tableaux/sum-som/101/cst01/famil19a-eng.htm, accessed January 19, 2014.

was not seen to be very different than the general population at 8.9 percent; however, taking into consideration the difference in regional living costs and nondiscretionary expenses, most of which were in the form of increased costs for medical care, the figure jumped to 15.9 percent, which was a 75 percent increase above the national rate.[2]

The average Canadian couple earned $88,220 in 2011. That number drops to $60,400 for an elderly couple and $32,800 for a single elderly female. Sadly, these elderly women were the primary caregivers for a spouse, and now they are left to care for themselves — typically on a reduced income. The median retired American couples' income was $45,763. The median income for males older than the age of 65 was $25,704, and $15,072 for females.

In Canada, after the death of a spouse, the survivor will lose the Old Age Security (OAS) income of the deceased spouse (up to $546.07 per month). Canada Pension Plan (CPP) survivor benefits will, at best, provide up to the maximum CPP benefit for a single person. If both partners had previously received the CPP and OAS maximums ($1,212.90 + $546.07), that is a total reduction in income of $1,758.97 per month, or $21,107.64 per year for the survivor. To make matters worse, if the deceased spouse was a member of a defined benefit pension plan, typically the survivor's benefit will be 66 percent of the amount previously paid to the deceased spouse.

American readers: Social Security benefits may be available to the survivor, similar to the Canadian Pension Plan, benefits are capped at the maximum for a single person. Eligibility is based on past earnings as well as year of birth. The Social Security website offers tools to explain survivors' benefits (www.ssa.gov/pubs/10077.html, accessed January 20, 2014).

It's no wonder your elderly parents may fear running out of money. Their best defense is to live within their budget and save money wherever they can.

1. Budget Tips for Seniors

Budgets are the backbone of any financial plan. The one thing the wealthy have in common with one another is their ability to consistently spend less than they make. Over time, the surplus money from

---

2 "A Profile of Older Americans: 2011" US Department of Health & Human Services Administration on Aging, accessed January 20, 2014. www.aoa.gov/Aging-Statistics/Profile/2011/docs/2011profile.pdf

their bank accounts is transferred to investment accounts, increasing net worth and wealth.

Now that your parents are approaching their later years, they may find their treasured nest egg is shrinking. They, and you (if you are their power of attorney), will want to get as much as possible for their hard-earned dollars. The following sections offer tips to help preserve their wealth and income.

1.1 Seniors' discounts

Always ask for the seniors' discount. Ensure your parents are doing so when shopping. You can help them by finding out when seniors' day is at the local grocery store or shopping mall, or what local restaurants have free coffee or other discounts for seniors.

1.2 Coverage and programs for seniors

Ensure your parents are always asking if an item or service is covered by Social Services, a health plan, a charity, or Veterans Affairs before they buy it so that they are not spending unnecessary funds. For example, walkers are subsidized when a health assessment is taken before purchase, which can save up to 90 percent of the cost. My mother-in-law had the assessment done and her walker cost her only $50 instead of $500!

If your parent is a veteran, he or she may qualify for assistance from Veterans Affairs. There are a wide variety of services for veterans and their families — programs designed to assist the veteran and his or her family after an injury, and many other services to help the veteran and his or her family throughout his or her life. Veteran assistance includes programs for the elderly including long-term care for end-of-life.

There is also the Veterans Independence Program (VIP) program, which helps veterans remain independent and self-sufficient in the home and existing community. Depending on your parent's circumstances and health needs, he or she may qualify for financial assistance to obtain services such as ground maintenance, housekeeping, personal care, access to nutrition, and health and support services provided by a health professional. VIP does not replace other federal, state, provincial, or municipal programs. Instead, its role is to complement existing programs to help meet a veteran's needs.

Community care access centers and other social organizations offer subsidized services for the elderly. There are many local, regional, state, and provincial programs designed to assist the elderly. Some are run by volunteers. You can find a service for almost every situation, from taxi service to shopping trips to someone who will play cards with your parent. Check your local community website and ask for services for the elderly.

Meals on Wheels is a low-cost option for seniors. The Meals on Wheels program delivers healthy meals (healthy especially when compared to the typical diet of the elderly) and is a great service to look into when your parents are unable to shop for and/or prepare their own meals. Found in communities all across North America, Meals on Wheels is a nonprofit program supported by many volunteers and organizations, so costs are kept low. Hot meals can be delivered for around $5 each, and frozen meals may be even less.

1.3 Government pensions

Social Security benefits are available to US residents who have worked and contributed during their careers. The maximum Social Security income for a 70-year-old American is $1,800 per month. The major source of income reported by 87 percent of older Americans in 2009 was Social Security. Social Security made up 90 percent or more of the income received by 35 percent of seniors.

With regard to Canadian government pension plans, if your parents rely on Canada Pension Plan (CPP) and Old Age Security (OAS) for the bulk of their income, they may qualify for the Guaranteed Income Supplement (GIS) that is available to low-income seniors. The GIS is available to residents of Canada who apply for it and who pass the annual taxable income test. The 2013 taxable income test for a single senior older than the age of 65 is $16,704. For a couple to meet the low-income test the maximum taxable income is $40,032.

If you recall in Chapter 4, the cash flow statement, we asked readers to segregate their interest, dividend, and capital gain income from the return of capital income. That is because a return of capital is *not* considered taxable income. It is possible for retirees to qualify for the GIS even when they may have substantial savings. Working with a financial advisor will help you to protect your parents' eligibility for the GIS. The financial advisor may recommend a change in the investment account to take advantage of the return of capital as a source of income.

With regards to the OAS clawback, if your parents' taxable income is higher than $70,954 (per person, at the time of writing), they will be subject to the OAS clawback. The OAS clawback is based on a sliding scale; the higher your taxable income, the more OAS is clawed back. Once taxable income exceeds $114,640, the OAS pension is completely eliminated. Take advantage of income splitting whenever one spouse has lower earnings. This will help to protect your parent at least in part from the OAS clawback. It is also possible to change the amount of taxable income paid by rebalancing your parents' investment portfolio. This should be done with the help of a qualified financial planner or investment advisor, as you would not want to trigger unnecessary fees or taxes in the process.

1.4 Canadian tax credits for seniors

If your parents are Canadian, they may also qualify for the following tax credits (current at the time of writing).

- **Age amount:** You can claim this amount the claimant is 65 years of age or older on December 31, and his or her net income is less than $78,684.

- **Income splitting:** Canadian residents receiving pension income from an employer may qualify for pension income splitting with a lower income spouse, which reduces the marginal tax rate of the higher income earner.

- **Pension income tax credit:** You may be able to claim up to $2,000 from the Federal Government if you reported eligible pension, superannuation, or annuity payments. Depending on your area of residence, you may qualify for an additional tax credit.

- **Transferring credits:** Find out if you can transfer the unused parts of certain nonrefundable tax credits that your spouse (or common-law partner) does not need. Canada Revenue Agency (CRA) does permit this for items such as the age amount, the pension amount, and the disability amount.

- **Family caregiver tax credit:** This credit is available to a family member, including a spouse, who cares for a dependent person due to impairment in physical or mental functions. You may be eligible to claim an additional $2,000. If you have more than one dependent at home, the credit can be claimed for each infirm relative.

- **Caregiver tax credit:** This is available to a family member other than a spouse.

- **Medical expenses:** Expenses in excess of approximately $2,000 (or 3 percent of net income, whichever number is lower) are deductible.

- **Attendant care:** Your elderly parents can generally claim the full amount for care in a full-time nursing facility or the salary of an attendant who cares for them at home.

- **Disability tax credit:** This tax credit works out to more than $1,100 and applies to expenses that might not qualify for the medical-expense tax credit (e.g., transportation or housing). There are many conditions for eligibility; see if you qualify by completing form T2201(www.cra-arc.gc.ca/E/pbg/tf/t2201/README.html) and answering the following simple questions:

  How long did your impairment last (or how long is it expected to last), and was it for a continuous period of at least 12 months?

  Does your impairment restrict you in one or more of the basic Activities of Daily Living?

  Do the effects of your impairment cause you to be markedly restricted all or substantially all of the time (at least 90 percent of the time) in one or more of the Basic Activities of Daily Living, even with appropriate therapy, medication, and devices?

- **Community volunteer income tax program:** CRA works with community organizers to connect low-income individuals who need help to complete their tax returns with volunteers.

- **Rent geared to income (RGTI):** Canada's regional governments provide RGTI for qualifying seniors. Housing is dedicated to assisting low- to moderate-income households with homes that are affordable and meet their needs. Special priority status (e.g., victims of violence fleeing abuse), health and safety priority status, or people with homeless status may be given higher priority. The elderly person may qualify for special priority if a case can be made for the safety of his or her current living arrangements. They must be able to demonstrate an ability to live independently, even if it is with the assistance of aids (e.g., walkers, wheelchairs), or home care. RGTI housing eligibility is based on taxable income. Waiting lists can be quite long. It's not uncommon to wait 12 to 36 months. If your parents qualify for the GIS, they have a good chance of qualifying for RGTI. Get their application in early.

1.4a Canadian actual income versus taxable income

You'll notice in the previous section that many amounts used to qualify for benefits are based on taxable income. To help clarify what this means, let's distinguish between actual and taxable income:

Taxable income is any income for which a T3, T4, or T5 is issued. Many elderly retirees receive income from their investment portfolios and if the investment is in a registered account, the income will be taxable. For those who have non-registered investments, some of the income they receive is in the form of return of capital. Some mutual funds are structured to pay out return of capital in the early years, while others structure a balance between return of capital and interest, dividends, and/or capital gains.

Prescribed life annuities (non-registered) are particularly well suited to keeping taxes down. For example, recently I asked for a life annuity quote for one of my clients. The investment amount the client was putting forward was $700,000. This would garner her a monthly income of $3,999, or a little less than $48,000 annually. The taxable income portion of this was only $10,900 annually. This is more tax efficient compared to earning 5 percent on the investment and paying tax on the full $35,000 of annual income! Even worse, if the client's investment were paid out to her as dividends rather than interest, the taxable income would have to be grossed up, affecting her ability to qualify for OAS and other government programs.

Dividends received from Canadian corporations receive preferential tax treatment through the application of the dividend tax credit; however, dividend income is the least income-friendly for retirees, since before a person can apply for this preferential treatment he or she must "gross up" the income. It is the grossed-up amount which is reflected as income on the tax return. This grossed-up amount is then used to determine eligibility for many income-tested benefits such as OAS, and the GIS. Dividends are grossed up by 138 percent; therefore a $1,000 dividend is grossed up to $1,380 for income tax reporting. Sample 9 shows the tax impact of a $1,000 income.

If you are your family member's primary caregiver, it is wise to build a team of professionals to assist you, including the person who currently prepares your parents' tax return (preferably an accountant versed in the benefits available to the elderly and the caregiver).

Sample 9
Tax Impact

Type of Investment Income	Income Reported on Tax Return	Tax Payable	After-Tax Income (assuming marginal tax rate of 40 percent)
GIC, Bonds, RRIF, Salary	$1,000	$400	$600
Dividends	$1,380	$250	$750
Capital Gains	$500	$200	$800
Income Mutual Fund with Return of Capital	-$400	$160	$840
Prescribed Life Annuity	-$15	$60	$940

Your parents' financial planner can be invaluable in projecting future income draws and the sustainability (how long the money will last) of your parents' investment portfolios. They can work with you to rebalance the investment portfolio to reduce taxation.

2. Joint Property and Accounts

During this financial planning process, many caregivers (non-spousal) and their parents choose to add the caregiver to the parents' bank and investment accounts as a joint owner. This may also apply to the family home or cottage. If you are the power of attorney (POA) for your parent and you are tempted do this, I caution you against doing so for the following reasons:

- Taxes must now be paid by both parties on whatever account, cottage, etc., you have become a joint holder. If the caregiver is in a higher tax bracket, he or she will not only owe taxes on funds earmarked for the parent, he or she will do so at a higher marginal tax rate. This applies to investments, cottages, any real estate other than the family home, and just about any asset on which there may be a capital gain, now or in the future.

- Changing an investment account or cottage to joint owner-ship will trigger taxation on unrealized capital gains to the parent. This may jeopardize cash flow for the year, as well as eligibility in Canada for OAS, GIS, and Rent Geared to Income. The capital gains laws in the US are similar in that property which is disposed of will trigger taxes if there is a capital gain (i.e., the property's fair market value is higher than the purchase price plus the cost of improvements). This refers to both investments and real estate.

- Joint holdings create questions around whose money or asset it is. Is the intent of the parent to simplify the payment of bills and manage the account? Or is the intent that the caregiver inherits the asset? In either case, at death, joint assets become the asset of the joint holder. This has caused more than one lawsuit; other family members may assert that the intent was to manage the asset, and that their fair share of the inheritance went to the caregiver.

The better alternative is to have POAs in place, and a will that clearly spells out who should get what, and what additional bequest would be to the caregiver, if any.

With the budgeting and planning knowledge you are building by reading this book, and the potential for even more expert advice from a team of professionals, you can do a great deal to ensure your parents' wealth lasts them through their remaining years and keeps them safe, comfortable, and happy in their surroundings.

chapter 6

Debt and the Elderly

Debt among the elderly is a climbing statistic. In the second quarter of 2013, senior debt increased by 6.5 percent; the highest jump of any age group.[1] According to the Certified Professional Consultants on Aging (CPCA), only 50 percent of seniors are mortgage-free, and 50 percent of seniors carry debt. Like oil and vinegar, debt and retirement do not mix well!

Current interest rates may provide retirees with a false sense of security. Everything may seem fine when the interest rate being charged is only 2 to 3 percent, inflation is running at 2 percent, and your investments are earning 5 percent (so you're basically breaking even). Consider, though, what would happen if interest rates increased by an additional 2 to 3 percent, and if inflation were to

---

1 "Are you betting on an inheritance to solve your money problems?," *Financial Post*, accessed January 20, 2014. business.financialpost.com/2013/10/25/are-you-betting-on-an-inheritance-to-solve-your-money-problems/?preview=true

simultaneously nudge up to 4 percent, and if the investment markets were to suffer another pullback, causing your portfolio to drop by 10 to 15 percent? I spell that T-R-O-U-B-L-E! Of course, the trouble with trouble is that once you are in it, it can be very hard to get out!

A recent Ipsos Reid survey[2] suggests debt is on the rise year-over-year for most people older than the age of 65. For example, in 2011, 69 percent of American households had some debt with the median debt at $70,000.[3] Those older than the age of 55 saw the largest relative increase in household debt. This group median debt increased by 64 percent over the year 2000 levels. The age 65 and older group was also the most likely to hold secured debt (e.g., mortgages) in 2011 relative to 2000. As for Canada in 2012, in Ontario the average household debt was up to $58,969, and in Alberta the number was even higher at $69,586. In both the US and Canada, debt levels among seniors is clearly on the rise. If you think your parents entered retirement with no debt, it might be time to think again.

The biggest concern with debt is that most elderly are on a fixed income. Mortgages and credit card debt charges can sneak up on us all, but when income is constant (as opposed to growing during the years of career advancement at work), it is very challenging to pay off the balance owing without jeopardizing future income sustainability.

I have met retirees who, having no other sources of investments, finance their debt with funds from tax-sheltered accounts. The concern here is that every dollar withdrawn from a registered account is subject to taxation. If you are withdrawing more than the required amount from registered accounts to service debt you are paying more taxes than needed. It is important to remember that Canadian tax laws require you to withdraw income from these sources at prescribed rates that force the holder to a zero balance by age 110. Americans must also withdraw a minimum income from their registered accounts. In the early years, assuming a minimum withdrawal, the retirement account balance will typically rise in value. However, by age 75 (or older), the increasing forced-withdrawal rate will now be higher than the rate of return, and the balance will continue to drop until there are no funds left. If more than the minimum is withdrawn to service debt, the holder will run out of money — perhaps decades too early!

---

2 "Younger Canadians Put Brakes on Debt in 2013, Older Keep Borrowing," TD Economics, accessed January 20, 2014. www.td.com/document/PDF/economics/special/YoungerCanadians PutBrakesOnDebtIn2012.pdf

3 "Household Debt in the US: 2000 to 2011," United States Census Bureau, accessed January 20, 2014. www.census.gov/people/wealth/files/DebtHighlights2011.pdf

Consider this example: Let's say your parents have a mortgage on their home that is being charged at a 4 percent interest rate, and the interest and principal repayments total $1,000 per month. To service this debt at a 30 percent tax rate, your parents are forced to withdraw $1,300 per month from their registered accounts ($1,000 to pay the mortgage and $300 to pay the taxes due). The true cost of this debt is therefore the 4 percent interest charge *plus* the additional taxes required to make the mortgage debt payment (30 percent).

Let's consider the same situation as above, but instead of a mortgage with a relatively low interest rate, let's work with credit card interest. Unlike a mortgage, credit cards charge very high interest rates! It is not uncommon to have a credit card with an 18 percent interest rate. Hopefully you do not need a financial calculator to be able to spell D-I-S-A-S-T-E-R! This would have serious implications for your parents' future financial welfare. The priority needs to be to pay off this debt as quickly as possible.

Supporting elderly parents' financial needs when they are in the low-income group is certainly not specific to North Americans. This is a global challenge that is growing every year. In late 2012, a law was passed in China requiring that family members who live separately from the elderly should visit them often, and that they should pay those elderly family members a monthly stipend if they live below the poverty line.[4]

If all children get involved early enough with the financial well-being of their parents, like you are doing by reading this book, the thoughtful and prudent planning you do will be sufficient to avoid you having to supplement their income with your own resources, and still ensure they are safe, healthy, and happy.

1. Reverse Mortgages

Another strategy that has become popular in recent years is the reverse mortgage. Typically, a reverse mortgage (also known as a "home equity conversion loan" or "home income plan") is a home equity loan that is made available to homeowners over a certain age (depending on the country where the person resides). Reverse mortgages may have gained popularity recently, but they are not a new concept. While they've only been around in Canada for about 10 years, they have been used in the US for more than 20 years, and in the UK for more than 50 years.

---

4 "What to do about your parents' debt," *Canadian Living*, accessed January 20, 2014. www.canadianliving.com/life/money/what_to_do_about_your_parents_debt.php

With a reverse mortgage, the homeowner is permitted to take a percentage of the value of his or her home (e.g., up to 50 percent) as tax-free cash. The amount of money you can receive is based on factors such as age, your spouse's age, the location of your home, and its current appraised value. Older seniors are eligible to receive a higher percentage of their home's value, while younger seniors get less. The average is about 33 percent.[5]

This cash can be provided as a single lump-sum payment, or in regular payments (e.g., monthly). The most tempting part of this transaction — in addition to the influx in cash flow — is that the homeowners do not have to make any payments on this cash until they choose to move or sell, and there are no income qualifications involved like there would be with a regular bank loan. For those with great discipline who can carefully plan how the money will be used to supplement their retirement income, it may be a constructive debt to take on.

Another benefit is that regardless of how much interest you accrue, you would never owe more than the house is worth when you sell it. This is called a "no-negative equity guarantee."

There can be a tax advantage to a reverse mortgage, given that it is considered a virtually nontaxable income stream, because while the income from the reverse mortgage is taxable, the interest that accumulates on the loan is deductible and usually offsets any tax payable.

If your parents want to leave the entire amount of their estate — including the asset value of their home — to their heirs, then a reverse mortgage is not the right option. It is designed to create additional cash flow but will ultimately cause a percentage of the home to have to be paid back upon sale (or death).

There are disadvantages along with the advantages, so let's explore those too. First and foremost, using a reverse mortgage requires the ability to remember that short-term decisions have long-term consequences. In other words, your parents will have to budget extremely well. The money needs to last. If your parents get it all in one lump sum, it is even more dangerous, as it can be tempting to take out more than they should at any given time. Discipline is the key with lump-sum payments, and not many people have that kind of discipline.

---

5 "Are reverse mortgages a good idea for retirees?" *The Globe and Mail*, accessed January 20, 2014. www.theglobeandmail.com/globe-investor/personal-finance/retirement-rrsps/the-pros-and-cons-of-reverse-mortgages/article12477397/#dashboard/follows/

The bigger downside, though, is that higher interest rates are involved. Borrowing money through a reverse mortgage costs more than doing so via other avenues (e.g., personal line of credit). Rates are low right now (2013), and can be locked in for up to five years, for example, but in those five years rates can easily double, putting the homeowner at risk when the term renews. While payments may not be required until selling the home, that doesn't mean no fees or interest charges are involved, so take those amounts into consideration as well. You'll be required to pay back the principal amount you borrowed, along with all the interest that accumulated over time. It's not "free" money, even though it might feel that way at first. It will take away from the value of the home as an asset because once you sell the home, the amount (plus interest) needs to be paid back right away, leaving less to use towards retirement home care or to bequeath to heirs.

It is also important to consider that at some point, the payments may max out, and a plan needs to be in place for that possibility as well. This is something that often necessitates the help of a qualified financial planner.

If married, before taking on a reverse mortgage, it is important to know that both spouses involved need to be listed as borrowers on the loan, because if only one of them is listed, the loan requires repayment immediately on the death of the spouse on the loan. That would leave the other spouse with none of the expected reverse mortgage income after that point, not to mention being forced to sell the home immediately.

Generally I am against reverse mortgages, as I believe that if things are so bad that you need to use a reverse mortgage, it is time to sell the house and downsize, rent, or move to a retirement home or into facility care. The family home can be seen as the asset of last resort, since the sale of the home frees up cash that can be used to fund your elderly family member's later years in a retirement home or facility care.

2. Real Estate Ownership

Over the years, I have watched several of my elderly clients sell the family home and purchase a condo, once they were no longer able to care for their home or themselves. In each case, they used up the funds from the sale of the home to purchase the condo. This left them with little or no additional funds from the sale of the home.

With all of their money now tied up in the condo, and no extra savings to draw on, these elderly clients found themselves in a position where they were constantly short of cash to meet their daily living requirements. The condo fees and property taxes alone would have gone a long way to paying the full price of rent in the same building! Clearly they would have been better off investing the proceeds from the sale of their home, and renting. The proceeds of the home could have been invested to provide the income required to meet the rent payment. As these elderly clients become less independent, and require assistance with the activities of daily living, they will likely be moving to a retirement residence within the next few years which will require the sale of the condo.

There is a solid argument to be made against the elderly owning real estate, especially when there is still debt on the property involved. Even if you think of it as an appreciating asset, once your parent reaches the elderly stage, there are not usually enough years to gain from an appreciating real estate market. Along with that, there is a very real risk of real estate values falling without having the luxury of time to wait for them to rebound.

If your parents are counting on the proceeds from selling their home to cover the costs of their later years in a retirement home, this plan could become problematic if real estate values drop significantly right at the time they need to sell. While housing prices all across North America have been appreciating consistently for the past decade and more, your parents will likely remember the drop in values that were experienced in the early 1980s.

The cost of renting, when compared to the cost of owning, can oftentimes be considerably less. When you factor in the cost of servicing any remaining debt/mortgage on the property, plus the operating and maintenance costs of a home, along with property taxes, it may be considerably more advantageous to your parents' budget to rent.

Finally, there are significant physical demands in maintaining a home, especially in areas where there are four seasons. From mowing the lawn all summer, to raking the leaves in the fall, to shoveling the driveway all winter, there is a need to be physically fit and active.

3. Leveraged Investments

By leveraged investments, I am referring to the process of borrowing money in order to invest it. Leveraged investments are mentioned here only because it has come to my attention that some retirees, including the elderly, have participated in this scheme. This is almost never a wise choice. Retirees do not meet the criteria for engaging in leveraged investments.

For the concept of leveraging to be successful, the cost of servicing the loan must be *less* than the investment earns. This requires that the money be invested in primarily equities. As you may know, equities offer the "potential" for higher returns, which is *not* a certainty!

The risk of the investments' value dropping is very real. Should the value drop, the interest payments on the original loan value must still be paid. Recent examples from 2007 and 2008, when there was a significant drop in the value of the typical portfolio, caused many financially challenging situations for retirees. Five years later, some investors from the 2007 to 2008 market downturn have yet to recover their losses. This strategy is not appropriate for people who need to draw income from the investment. Many investors become very emotional during market downturns and cash in investments they own that are losing money in the short-term, rather than wait for the market to recover.

In addition, people fail to take into account the likelihood of an increase in interest rates being charged, increasing the cost of carrying the loan.

When looking at leveraged investments, financial planning guidelines suggest that the investor meets three criteria:

1. The client has a high tolerance for market risk and is a sophisticated investor.

2. The client has a long time line (i.e., ten years or longer) to allow time for the market to recover if there is a drop in value.

3. The client has high income and is in the highest marginal tax rate so that he or she can take advantage of the tax relief on the interest payments for the loan involved, and so that he or she can pay the interest costs with cash flow.

Most retirees, particularly those who are elderly, would not meet any of the above three criteria. To add to these three, clients should not rely on taking income from a leveraged investment. In my experience when I have come across seniors who are leveraging, they were relying on the income from the leveraged loan and hoping the investment would make more than the interest charged. As a result, some of their advisors are facing lawsuits! Ultimately, leveraging at this stage of life is simply a bad idea.

Tying back into the reverse mortgage discussion, I do not recommend using any lump-sum payments gained through a reverse mortgage to invest in equities with the hopes of earning a higher interest rate of return than the loan payment. An annuity purchase might work with those funds, especially if it has a return-of-capital guarantee, but caution would still be required. At present, some of the interest involved in buying a nonprescribed annuity is tax deductible, but for prescribed annuities, none of the interest is tax deductible. As you can see, the complexities involved require the assistance and advice of a qualified financial planner to ensure you are maximizing all the tax benefits.

My final words on this: It is *never* advisable for the elderly to enter into a leveraged investment. I consider it bad enough to qualify as elder abuse, if not fraud. Does it sound like I feel strongly about this topic?

4. Taking Action

It is never too soon to start exploring your parents' debt and see where they stand. Worksheet 8 is a list of questions to start asking and action steps to take in order to get the full and accurate picture.

Your local bank can work with you to help consolidate the debt from multiple sources into one loan that has a lower interest rate. For example, if your parent has multiple credit card balances being charged at 18 percent interest, it would be far more financially beneficial to use a personal line of credit (at a far lower interest rate) to pay off the cards, and then make payments to the line of credit until it is paid off.

Another option is to work with a credit consolidation agency. If you go this route, it is essential to shop around and ensure you are getting the best interest rate. Even better, you should work with your financial planner to come up with the best options. In the USA, you can contact the Association of Independent Consumer Credit Counseling Agencies (AICCCA). The AICCCA is a member-sponsored national association representing not-for-profit credit counseling companies providing consumers with credit counseling, debt management, and financial education (www.aiccca.org). In Canada, you can reach out to a nonprofit group such as Consolidated Credit Counseling Services of Canada (www.consolidatedcredit.ca) for assistance.

Worksheet 8
Gathering Debt Information

1. How much debt do your parents have? Collect all the details about their outstanding loans, credit cards (including interest being charged), and the term of all loans.

2. What kind of debt is involved? Gain clarity as to whether it is mortgage, bank credit cards, department store credit cards, personal loans, etc.

3. Look at the impact of interest charges. Calculate how much total interest charges were paid in the last year. How significant is that amount when compared as a percentage of their income?

4. Get any existing debt under control as soon as possible by paying it down, eliminating high interest charge cards, consolidating cards and, as power of attorney, stepping in and canceling cards and/or changing the PIN when your parent lacks the capacity to exercise the required restraint to avoid incurring unnecessary charges.

5. Protecting Your Parents from Fraud and Financial Abuse

One of the ways seniors can incur debt or suffer unplanned and un-expected financial setbacks is fraud and financial abuse. The elderly are particularly susceptible to unscrupulous requests for monies, both from family members and friends as well as unknown fraudsters.

Empower and educate your elderly parents by talking to them about these potential situations of fraud and financial abuse:

- **Door-to-door sales fraud:** Be on the lookout for people who come to the home suggesting they can perform a service (e.g., repairs) and pressure you to provide a check or cash deposit right away before they get started. Ask your parent to call you or a trusted family member before agreeing to anything.

- **Credit card fraud:** Make sure you or your parent are review-ing all credit card purchases on their monthly statement and verifying the purchases were made by your parent, and not a family member or friend. If your parent has memory prob-lems already, suggest that all credit card shopping receipts be placed in a drawer or file each day so that they can be referenced later for comparison with the statement.

- **Investment fraud:** Be wary of anyone who offers to "double your money" or offers quick gains with a new investment or idea, and requests funds from your parent to do so. Quick or large profits can never be guaranteed, and those offering guarantees are suspicious.

- **Lottery fraud:** Seniors may be tempted to believe lottery scams that tell them via telephone, Internet, or mail that they've won a large prize and that all they need to do to claim it is send a check for "handling fees" in order to receive it. With memory challenges, they could easily be talked into thinking they've just "forgotten" that they entered the contest in the first place. Have them touch base with you before they take any action to claim a prize.

- **Email requests for money:** A common scam in recent years involves setting up a fake email account representing a friend or family member of the senior, and requesting "emergency funds" to help them out of a difficult situation. A common theme involves saying they have had their wallet stolen while on vacation and need money to get back home. Ensure your parent knows they should double check with you or another family member to verify the story before taking action. Note that this also happens by phone and via social networking programs (e.g., Facebook) where accounts have been hacked.

- **Family abuse or misuse:** As hard as it is to accept, the reality is that many seniors suffer financial abuse at the hands of their loved ones. It is important to talk to your parents about this possibility, and help them guard against unauthorized use of their bank cards, credit cards, assets, property, cash, or checks. Keeping those items in a secure and secretive location is a good first step toward protecting them. You will also want to guard against people putting pressure on your parent to change their will or sign any legal documents they might not understand, or staying with your parent in their home without contributing to expenses such as rent or utilities.

- **Telephone scams:** A recent scam is for fraudsters to call and say they work for the government (e.g., Social Security, Canada Pension Plan). They will tell the person that payments will be stopped unless he or she gives them his or her personal account information. Many people panic when they think it is a government institution calling so they willingly give up personal account numbers and information. Tell your parent to ask for their contact information, but do not give any personal information over the phone. After hanging up, find the number to the government agency in the *phone book* and call to ask if someone from the agency is indeed calling. If not, report the call to their fraud department.

In all of the above instances, the fraud and/or theft should be reported to your local police.

chapter 7

Investing Your Parents' Savings

Now that you know what monies your parents currently have, along with income they'll be receiving in the future, and you have a plan to take care of any debt, it's time to think about how you will invest the rest.

The goal of this chapter is to help you, or the power of attorney (POA), make wise choices that will lead you to handle investments with confidence. Like any other long-end-game, successful investing requires that we adhere to a few common principals.

Before we begin, let's review the common traits of successful portfolio design for retirees. In section **5.**, you will find three sample portfolios:

1. Pre-retirees' portfolio
2. Early retirees' portfolio

3. Late retirees' portfolio

Each portfolio will focus on successful strategies for the target retiree. All three will follow the same principles. The three key things to remember:

- Know what you can control and control what you can.
- R-I-S-K is a four-letter word.
- Rule of 100.

The following sections will discuss these key points in detail.

1. Control

In life, as in investing, a common reason we get into trouble is when we try to control what cannot be controlled, and fail to control what we can. As an advisor, I quickly learned that I could not control interest rates, currency fluctuations, or the markets. All of these things are influenced by forces beyond our control, and at any given time, the "experts" will have differing viewpoints.

A good example of this, at the time of writing, is the experts telling us that interest rates will soon be going up. The reasons given often make a lot of sense: we are at (or near) an all-time low for historic interest rates, the economy is recovering, and job growth is taking place. The countering argument is that our governments (locally and around the world) have the highest debt levels on record, so if interest rates are to rise significantly, this will make it more expensive for them to pay their debt and lead to a call for increased taxation, less consumer spending, and so on. Who is right? Even the so-called experts do not know.

1.1 What is in your control?

Keep a clear picture of your goals in your mind, and make the small decisions that will lead you ever closer to those goals. You *can* control the strategies you employ to protect yourself. A little common sense applied to the choices can go a long way. Keep the end game in mind and make strategic investment and product decisions to maximize desired results.

You *can* control, at least to some extent, the amount of taxes that will need to be paid by allocating monies to the investment accounts that will shield you from taxation and/or a loss of benefits.

You *can* control which of your parents' accounts income will be drawn from first. For example, in Canada before the age of 71, it is possible to draw income from your non-registered accounts, keeping your RRSPs tax-sheltered for longer. Or, if waiting until age 71 will cause you to be in a substantially higher tax bracket, you may choose to draw income from your Registered Retirement Saving Plans as soon as you retire. The good news is that you may choose to draw income from the sources that preserve the most wealth.

Another factor you *can* control is who will manage your parents' accounts. Will you be making the investment choices or will you work with a financial planner or an investment advisor? Even if you feel confident, and you are already managing your own investments as a do-it-yourself project, this is not a prudent choice. After all, this is your parents' money and you have a responsibility to protect their assets, track the rate of returns, and provide and manage cash flow. If your parents are still competent, you will be providing them with regular reports, and you may be asked to provide updates to other family members. You could choose to work with your parents' existing advisor; I would recommend this approach, at least until you are satisfied the advisor has your parents' best interests at heart and is diligent in the care of your parents' wealth. If your parents do not have a financial planner, you may want to introduce them to your own advisor. If neither you nor your parents are currently working with a financial planner, or you are unsatisfied with the current advisor, read Chapter 11 for information about selecting a team of professionals. There you will learn what to look for in a financial planner.

When working with a financial advisor, you can help yourself by listening closely to the advisor's investment strategy and ensure it matches your parents' goals. You can guide the advisor in the selection of investments by insisting on investments that meet the following criteria. Choose investments that offer a combination of the following:

- Consistently good track history, not less than five years; ideally, a ten-year history or more.
- Low volatility when compared to their peer group.
- When choosing between a shortlist of similar investments that satisfy the first two characteristics, choose the ones with the lower fees.

Keep your eye on fees, as your knowledge of what fees apply to each investment product can help you control those costs as well. Whether you actively trade stocks, bonds, and exchange traded funds (ETFs), or hold mutual funds or segregated funds, there are associated costs. Stocks, bonds, and ETFs are traded on the securities market, so each purchase and sale triggers a fee (commission) for the advisor. If there are many transactions, these fees can be significant. In addition to paying for the purchase and sale of ETFs, know that ETFs also have built-in management fees, though these fees are usually lower than those of a mutual fund.

Mutual funds and segregated funds report the rate of return *after* all fees. Both charge management fees to manage the funds, pay associated costs, and pay the financial advisor a commission. You, the investor, may not be aware of these fees unless you ask. For example, fund A had a 6 percent rate of return last year and the embedded management fees and commissions were 2 percent, meaning this fund actually earned 8 percent before fees. Assuming you were able to identify the same fund with a fee of 1.5 percent your rate of return would have been 6.5 percent. This may not be as difficult as you imagine. Do not be afraid to ask, if the same (or a similar) fund you are holding is available with a lower fee. Often the same fund is available in differing "classes," some of which may have a lower fee structure.

Many fund companies offer what basically amounts to a volume discount. The more money you invest with them, the lower your fees. By consolidating your assets and accounts, it is possible to achieve significant savings. Better yet, some fund companies will allow you to pool both your and your parents' accounts as a "family," thereby allowing both you and your parents to benefit from the lowest possible fees. Typically, volume discounts are available for accounts of more than $250,000, $500,000, and $1 million, with each level offering a lower fee than the level before. Be sure to ask your financial planner if you and your family qualify for reduced fees based on the size of your combined accounts.

If you or your parents currently hold investments with various banks or financial institutions, you may want to consider consolidating all investments with a single financial planner you trust. Not only will it be possible to benefit from lower fees, the financial planner will view your account as more valuable, and will increase his or her services to match your importance to his or her practice. Another advantage when working with a single financial planner, rather than a hodgepodge of advisors, is that this primary contact will know the most about you and your family, and will work towards providing you with advice customized to your unique family needs.

2. Risk

Let's explore the concept of risk in retirement. Retirees face four forms of risk during retirement:

1. **Longevity risk:** We talked a little about longevity risk in the last chapter. With people now living longer than previous generations, it is quite possible to be retired for many decades. The probability of a healthy 65-year-old female living to age 80 is now 81 percent! This means that 81 percent of women who are currently age 65 need to plan their retirement nest egg to last until at least age 80. Of course, we would not want to run out of money the day after our 80th birthday, since 44 percent of this group is expected to live to age 90.

   Let's take my client Grace, age 65, as an example. She has $100,000 in her investment account, and she earns 5 percent interest on that amount annually. She draws $6,500 per year. By age 92, her account balance will be zero. To earn that 5 percent, she had to take some market risk. Grace does not like risk, though, and so she decided instead to invest in bonds. Her return is now more secure, although it averages just 2.5 percent returns. With the safer investment, Grace will run out of money in her early 80s.

2. **Inflation risk:** Since we have been in a low-inflation environment for many years now it is easy to forget how inflation can cut into our ability to purchase the same basket of goods over the years. Assuming a 3 percent rate of inflation, the cost of purchasing a cart full of groceries would double in 20 years. Investments that do not keep up with inflation will mean a loss in purchasing power over time.

3. **Liquidity risk:** Some investments are less "liquid" than others, meaning they may take a long time to sell (liquidate). Real estate is a good example of an investment that, even in good markets, takes time to liquidate. Ninety days or longer is a typical time frame. In a bad real estate market such as the recent drop experienced in the USA, during the worst of the real estate meltdown, some properties could not be sold

at *any* price. Annuities could also be said to be illiquid, since once the purchase has been made, it cannot be undone.

4. **Market volatility risk:** The financial markets have, and will continue to, experience ups and downs. The most recent pull-back was in 2008. For those who were fully invested in equities in 2008, their portfolio may still not have fully recovered. Poor market returns during retirement may have a dramatic impact on your retirement income.

The major difference between the portfolios of younger investors (who have ten or more years before retirement), and those who will be, or are already retired, is the ability to withstand market risk. Younger investors, who have a long time left working and are making regular (monthly) contributions to their investment portfolios, may be able to recover from loss in their investments and are therefore typically less concerned with risk. Rather, this group seeks to maximize returns. In doing so, they are prepared to take on risk in the hopes the result will be a higher rate of return over time. With time on their side, and assuming they do not withdraw money until retirement, they are likely to do just fine.

Investors who are nearing retirement or are already retired do not have the luxury of waiting for their investments to recover from market loss. Imagine for a moment that you retired in January of this year with a portfolio value of $400,000. You plan to withdraw 5 percent ($20,000) in December of each year. During the year, the markets drop and your portfolio suffers a loss of 25 percent ($100,000). Does this seem extreme? Just think back to 2008 when the S&P 500 lost 37 percent in 2008 alone! It's not inconceivable at all! Your new portfolio balance is now $300,000. What percent do you now need to draw to withdraw $20,000? That would be 7 percent! It gets worse, because even if your portfolio earns 5 percent each year thereafter, and you continue to withdraw $20,000 per year, it will still be on an ever-declining balance! What can you do? In life, as in your investment portfolio, you can choose to avoid, manage, transfer, or eliminate risk.

- **Avoid:** Avoid risk by choosing less risky investments. Read on about the Rule of 100 for more clarification on this topic (see section **3.**).

- **Manage:** Accept that investing poses some risks, and be smart enough to manage those risks via a well-diversified portfolio.

Diversification, both by asset and by product, is crucial to creating a sustainable and safe investment plan for retirement. In section **4.** you will find a list of investment products that are suitable for retirement. Assets fall into the categories of cash, fixed income, and equities. The type of products in each asset class can further be broken down as well.

Cash can consist of actual cash, or products that can be readily converted to cash such as money market, Guaranteed Investment Certificates (GICs), and Treasury Bills (t-bills). A t-bill is a short-term debt obligation backed by the US government with a maturity of less than one year. Fixed-income products include short- and long-term bonds. Equities include individual common stocks and preferred shares. Mutual funds, segregated funds, variable annuities, and exchange traded funds may hold any combination of the above.

- **Transfer:** It is possible to transfer the risk of loss in your portfolio to a third party by purchasing insurance for your investments. Variable annuities sold by insurance companies work like a mutual fund but offer income guarantees.

- **Eliminate:** Choose investments that have no risk at all. GICs eliminate the risk of loss of capital, but remember that risk comes in many forms. By providing protection from loss of capital, when measured as a protection against inflation, GICs would score very low.

Review Sample 10, comparing differing investment products and their ability to achieve retirees' goals.

It quickly becomes apparent that the best way to manage all four forms of risk is to take the "Goldilocks" approach: A little of this, a little of that, and mix until it is "just right." In fact, that is what many of us in the financial planning profession do to help retirees and the elderly see their money last longer. My favorite book on the subject of risk is *Against the Gods: The Remarkable Story of Risk* by Peter L. Bernstein (Wiley, 1998).

3. The Rule of 100

You know what they say about "old wives" tales: The reason they persist is because they have merit. Well, this old wives tale is called the Rule of 100. What is the Rule of 100? Just take your age, subtract it from 100, and this now forms the basis of basic asset allocation.

Sample 10
Investment Products

Retirement Goal	Annuity	GICs	Variable Annuity	Mutual Fund Balanced Stock/Bond Portfolio
Liquidity: Ability to make unscheduled withdrawals	N/A	High	High with a possible penalty	High
Guaranteed Lifetime Income	High	N/A	High	N/A
Simplicity: Product is easy to manage and understand	High	High	Medium	Medium
Protection from Inflation Does investment keep pace with inflation?	Low	Low	Medium	High

Asset allocation, in essence, involves placing your assets into distinct product categories to help provide a sustainable retirement income while also minimizing risk. Even if your parent does not have a pension, the right mix of investment products can act similarly, providing regular payments to him or her throughout his or her retirement.

Consider the following:

- At age 50, you could be considered a **pre-retiree**. Your asset allocation would be balanced, with 50 percent of your investment funds in equities and 50 percent in fixed-income products.

- At age 70, you could be considered an **early retiree**. Your asset allocation would be moderate, so the fixed income portion of your portfolio increases to 70 percent with equities forming the remaining 30 percent.

- At age 80, you could be considered a **late retiree**. Your asset allocation is conservative now, so the fixed-income portion of your portfolio now increases to 80 percent with equities forming the remaining 20 percent.

Of course, from here a financial planner will make many more adjustments to include investments that provide guaranteed income, bonds, dividend-paying stocks, global assets, infrastructure, real estate, and emerging markets.

Common characteristics of pre-retirees' and retirees' portfolios include:

- Transition from a portfolio in which assets are accumulated to one where income is produced.
- An emphasis on *value* versus *growth* stocks.

Think of well-known, successful investor and businessman Warren Buffett. Mr. Buffett has always shied away from high-tech companies, not only because he finds it hard to understand how they make a profit, but also because they do not pay dividends. Mr. Buffett, similar to the retirees I know, likes to get paid to have others hold his investments!

In section **5.**, you'll find three sample portfolios, one for each type of retiree mentioned above.

4. Products Suitable for Retirees

The following sections describe the products suitable for retirees.

4.1 Guaranteed Investment Certificates (GIC)

Guaranteed Investment Certificates (GICs) (also referred to as "term deposits") offer a guaranteed interest rate for a predetermined (fixed) period of time and are most often issued by banks or trust companies. While they don't have the potential for the high returns of riskier investments such as stocks and equities, they do have the benefit of low risk. GICs may be purchased in a "GIC ladder"; a series of GICs are purchased, each one with a maturity date one year longer than the previous one. Forming a "ladder" of maturity effectively staggers income for the duration of the ladder.

4.2 Bonds

Bonds are debt securities in which the issuer agrees to pay interest for borrowing money. Bonds, similar to GICs, have a maturity date. Interest is usually payable at fixed intervals (e.g., annually), and the security of the bond (how low-risk it is) depends on the rating the issuer is given. Bonds can be issued by governments or corporations. A bond with a rating of AA or AAA indicates a very high credit-quality, whereas a bond with a rating of BB, C, or lower indicates it has low-credit quality and is at more risk for default. Bonds may be purchased in a "bond ladder" similar to the GIC ladder in section **4.1.** Alternatively, investors may purchase a diversified portfolio of bonds through mutual, segregated funds, or exchange traded funds (ETFs).

4.3 Life annuities

Sold through a life insurance company, life annuities offer retirement income for life at a preset amount. The investors or retirees give the financial institution or insurance company a lump sum payment in exchange for a series of regular income payments, the duration of which is based on how long the purchaser will live; after death no further payments are made (newer versions offer a return of capital guarantee, if purchased at the time).

Life annuities can be purchased based on the life of an individual or on the life of a couple, with payments continuing until the last death. Once purchased, they cannot be reversed. This product could be considered "longevity insurance" as payments are guaranteed no matter how long you live. Not to be overlooked are the tax advantages of life annuities when purchased with non-registered funds.

4.4 Mutual funds

A mutual fund is a professionally managed group of investments tied together in one fund. They can involve a variety of investment products including stocks and bonds, and the person or team who manages the fund is responsible for deciding what holdings are purchased by the fund. There are management fees involved regardless of performance, which are susceptible to market fluctuations.

4.5 Segregated funds

Canadian insurance companies offer this type of investment fund. Segregated funds are similar to mutual funds, offering the growth potential of a mutual fund but with a component of insurance. The insurance component is the guarantee to the policy holders, including such things as reimbursement of capital on death, or at maturity of the contract, even if the investment has lost money. Other benefits include the ability to name a beneficiary, thereby avoiding probate (the funds would flow directly to the named beneficiary). They also offer some measure of creditor protection. The term "segregated" is used to express that the fund is fully segregated from the company's general investment funds; something required by law in Canada.

4.6 Variable annuities

Variable annuities are a recent hybrid combining the features of a life annuity along with the features of mutual funds. Similar to a life annuity, variable annuities are sold through a life insurance company. Also similar to an annuity, they provide a guaranteed lifetime income, even if the account balance should drop to zero. The payments received from a variable annuity are guaranteed by contract at a preset percent of the deposit amount, based on the age at which you begin to take income. Like a mutual fund, variable annuities allow you to invest in various investment funds, which will fluctuate with the market. There is potential for the funds to grow and you retain the ability to change the underlying funds, to withdraw funds beyond the guaranteed amount (subject to a penalty), or to completely close the account and take the market value of your investment in cash. These offer an exciting potential for seniors who want to have their cake and eat it too, so understandably the fees are higher for variable annuities than for mutual funds. Part of the higher fee goes to pay for the insurance rider, which is typically 1 percent.

If you or your elderly parents already own variable annuities, great care should be taken before canceling these contracts, as once canceled, they may not be able to be replaced. Many of the best variable annuities were closed to new deposits after the 2007 to 2008 market correction. This was done to protect the owners of these contracts.

4.7 Dividends

Some stocks (also known as equities) pay dividends during the period that you are holding them in your account, and have the potential to increase in value if the underlying company is doing well. Dividends can be a good source of regular income. They are not guaranteed. It is important to purchase dividend-paying stocks from companies that have a good track record of paying dividends during both bad and good times. Only purchase the stocks of those companies that have a solid financial standing and are paying out less in dividends than they earn. Just like your own personal budget and expense sheet, the amount they pay out needs to be less than the amount they take in. This is called a "payout ratio." Dividend mutual funds provide professional money management and diversification, making them a safer choice than individual dividend-paying stocks.

4.8 Exchange traded funds (ETFs)

Exchange traded funds (ETFs) are a group of investments that track an index, such as a stock exchange (e.g., Toronto Stock Exchange). Since they are not actively managed by professional money managers, they typically have lower management fees than traditional mutual funds, although this lack of management also means they are generally more volatile than mutual funds.

There are many other products available, as well as differing versions of similar products, such as T class funds that offer tax sheltering, or pooled funds offering reduced fees. It is best to speak to your financial advisor about the ones that will suit you and your family's situation best.

5. Sample Portfolios

The following sections describe the three different types of sample portfolios for retirees.

5.1 Pre-retiree's portfolio

A pre-retiree's portfolio is designed for the typical 50-year-old who plans to retire in the next 10 to 15 years. This portfolio will be divided equally between income and equities, 50/50. Your 50s are your last chance to bulk up your savings before retiring. This is the time to set a goal for the ultimate size of your nest egg at retirement and to think about how the new deposits you make are to be allocated in order to achieve the 50 percent income and 50 percent equity mix you need for this stage of life.

This balanced approach puts you in a good position to benefit from market upswings, while the fixed-income assets offer some downside protection. The equity portion can be further broken down into local, national, and foreign equities. Canadian readers would use Canadian funds for their local allocation. For American readers, the majority allocation would be in US equities, and foreign equities would be any equity allocation outside your country of residence.

The focus on the equity side should be towards investments that pay a dividend. Specialty funds should form no more than 10 percent of the total portfolio.

A pre-retiree's portfolio would look like this:

- 10 percent cash
- 40 percent fixed income
- 30 percent (local or national equity)
- 20 percent foreign equity

5.2 Early retiree's portfolio

The early retiree's portfolio is designed for the young and active re-tiree. This portfolio of 60 to 70 percent fixed income and 30 to 40 percent equities is designed to produce a tax-efficient income stream in retirement. The most common fear of the newly retired is running out of money so the aim is to avoid that.

The backbone of this portfolio may be a life annuity or a variable annuity with a lifetime income guarantee. Annuities can be used to ensure your basic monthly operating costs are covered. If you seek more information on what an annuity and variable annuities are, re-visit section **4.**

Example: Your monthly operating costs (i.e., home, transporta-tion, insurance, food) are $3,000 a month. Your guaranteed income from all sources (e.g., pension plans) is $2,500 a month. That is a $500 per month shortfall. By purchasing a life annuity that pays you $500 a month, you are assured your basic needs will be provided for.

Because life annuities are illiquid and do not offer inflation pro-tection, consider limiting (at this time) your allocation of annuities to 30 percent or less of your total investable assets. Variable annu-ities offer more liquidity, but these too should be only purchased if you are planning to keep them for the long term. The remainder of your investable assets can now be invested to provide for the fun things in life, such as travel and entertainment.

In addition to providing a secure income stream for as long as you live, life annuities are extremely tax efficient when purchased with non-registered funds. For example, the purchase of a $100,000 life annuity at age 70 may produce annual income in excess of $8,000, of which $550 is taxable. The remaining $7,450 is a return of capital.

Compare this to a $100,000 GIC paying 2 percent interest therefore providing you with $2,000. The entire $2,000 of annual income would be taxable!

When selecting investments that pay out income in the form of dividends, it is important to compare the amount being paid out with the actual amount earned by the investment. This may seem straightforward, but it is possible for funds (stocks) to have a higher payout ratio than what has actually been earned. A good choice is a fund that has a 4 to 5 percent payout ratio but earns 6 to 7 percent; that way the account balance will continue to increase and the income will be sustainable.

In Canada, dividends in non-registered accounts can create a problem for seniors by increasing their taxable income which affects OAS clawbacks and GIS eligibility. One strategy is to move dividend-paying assets into registered accounts, and move GICs, bonds, and other interest-bearing assets into non-registered accounts. This works because the dividend tax gross-up increases the taxable income to 138 percent of dividends being paid, whereas interest income is taxed at 100 percent. This makes a lot of sense, but is an idea that may be missed by financial or investment advisors who are more accustomed to working with clients who are still in the workforce and younger than 65.

This is a good time to review your parents' investments with a financial planner to ensure they are on target and your parents have the means to support themselves to a ripe old age.

An early retiree's portfolio would look like this:

- 25 percent life annuity or variable annuity
- 10 percent cash and/or GIC
- 35 percent fixed income
- 20 percent (local or national equities)
- 10 percent foreign equities

5.3 Late retiree's portfolio

The major focus of a late retiree's portfolio is capital preservation. This is the stage of life when your parents may be considering moving to a retirement home. It is highly likely that less money will be spent on travel and entertaining. Even though recreational costs will go down, be aware that other costs may be taking their place such as medications, health-care services, or retrofitting their home for improved safety. By this time, the original retirement nest egg may be diminishing. Consideration may be given to purchasing another life annuity, or simply to increasing the cash and/or GIC component of the portfolio. The foreign equity portion of the portfolio may be further reduced, as foreign equities can be more volatile than local or national equities.

It is important to note that some products are no longer available to those older than a certain age (typically age 80 to 85). This limitation includes segregated funds. The advantage of segregated funds is they have guaranteed death benefits and the ability to avoid probate. A beneficiary can be named so funds can flow directly to the beneficiary rather than the estate.

Before your parent reaches the age of 80 it is a good idea to sit down with a financial planner who can help you project future costs, calculate how long the nest egg will last, and consider whether annuities or segregated funds should be added to the portfolio mix.

A late retiree's portfolio would look like this:

- 30 percent life annuity or variable annuity
- 15 percent cash and/or GIC
- 45 percent fixed income
- 10 percent equities

Note: Variable annuities, segregated funds, and/or combination mutual funds can be used to satisfy the fixed income.

Now it's time to review your elderly parents' existing portfolio and the asset allocation therein. Compare it to the sample portfolios. This is a good way to gain an appreciation of whether your parents' portfolio is too aggressive or too conservative. Unless you have had a lot of experience investing your own monies, it is wise to consult with a financial planner who has experience working with retirees, and the elderly specifically. In Chapter 11, we will provide some guidelines for hiring the professional advisors who can best help you.

As we close out this chapter, remember that as the power of attorney (POA) for your elderly parent, you are expected to keep track of all investment returns, cash flow, and all fees associated with the investment portfolio. Many people find it helpful to create a tracking binder or a file on their computer to ensure that this information does not get lost and can be shared with other family members as required.

chapter 8

Insurance for Seniors

You may have thought that once your parents are retired, there will no longer be a need for insurance. The truth is there are many applications and benefits to owning insurance. In this chapter, we will cover the basic types of insurance that are most frequently used in our golden years.

While you are reading this chapter, I suggest you think about your parents' existing insurance plans and how they fit into their overall financial plan. These are some of the questions you will need to ask:

- Is there a gap in your parents' insurance coverage?

- What is the best use for older policies already in place, and what changes, if any, should be made?

- Are the beneficiary designations up to date? Does there need to be a change of beneficiary?

- What additional coverage would you like to explore with a licensed life agent?

1. Reasons to Purchase Life Insurance

I often consider the Swiss Army Knife of financial plans to be life insurance because it has everything to cover almost every situation. The following sections include several reasons seniors purchase life insurance.

1.1 Expenses

The most straightforward reason to purchase life insurance as a senior is to pay for last expenses such as a funeral and any costs of settling the estate.

1.2 Cash flow and estate preservation

Life insurance can increase cash flow, improving the person's lifestyle during retirement, while ensuring an inheritance. This concept is called a back-to-back annuity and life insurance policy, taken out at the same time and for the same amount.

Assuming the senior is in good health, the back-to-back approach works well with a last-to-die policy on a couple. Sample 11 compares the after-tax income of a back-to-back annuity and life insurance policy in the amount of $270,000 with the purchase of a Guaranteed Income Certificate (GIC) in the same amount.

Greg is 73 years of age and his wife Holly is 68 years old. As you can see in Sample 11, Greg and Holly are far better off with the back-to-back annuity and life insurance policy than they would be had they purchased a GIC — $8,798 per year ahead, to be exact. Now, if they did not have children, or had no interest in leaving their children an inheritance, they might choose to simply purchase the life annuity. The reason they — and many other seniors — choose to purchase a life policy is because they want to leave their children an inheritance. Clearly, if Greg and Holly chose to draw an income of $23,517 per year from a $270,000 investment, in time there would be a zero balance. The back-to-back strategy is a win-win for Greg, Holly, and their children.

1.3 Pension maximization

A life insurance policy is purchased to replace the loss of income from pensions when the higher-income earning spouse passes away.

Sample 11
Comparison of an After-Tax Income of a Back-to-Back Annuity and Life Insurance Policy

	Deposit	Annual	ROR*
Annuity income	$ 270,000.00	$ 23,517.00	9%
Insurance premium $270K policy		$7,588.00	3%
Income after paying premium		$ 15,929.00	6%
Taxable portion		$ 5,161.00	
Assumed tax rate 33%		$ 1,703.20	
Net Income After Tax (and insurance policy)		$ 14,225.80	

Compare to a GIC 3% Interest Rate

	Deposit	Annual Income	ROR*
Compare to GIC at 3% $ 270,000.00	270,000.00	$ 8,100.00	3%
Taxable Income from GIC		$ 8,100.00	
Assumed Tax Rate		$ 2,673.00	
Net Income After Tax		$ 5,427.00	

Back-to-Back Annual After-Tax Income Advantage

Back-to-Back Net Income After Tax (and insurance policy)		$ 14,225.80	
GIC Net Income After Tax		$ 5,427.00	
Advantage (after all costs including tax)		$ 8,798.80	

*Note: ROR stands for Rate of Return.

In 2011, the average retired couple earned $63,800 before taxes, and the average elderly female earned just $32,800. The reason for that drop can be explained by the loss of the second person's government pension income that is no longer available when a spouse dies, and the reduction in benefits from defined benefit pension plans (usually a reduction of 30 percent or more). Life insurance helps to protect the income and lifestyle of the surviving spouse.

1.4 Estate planning

There are many reasons seniors may want to enhance their estate values. The most common reason is to offset taxes due on the estate. These reasons most frequently take one of two forms:

- Business owners or investors with large holdings in real estate (e.g., family cottage, rental properties) may face a huge tax bill on their death forcing them to sell the business and rental properties under duress. Life insurance creates the liquidity needed to meet the tax obligation on time.

- Registered Retirement Savings Plans are fully taxable on the second death (i.e., when the second spouse dies), so many seniors like to offset the tax bill with a life insurance policy. There are several ways to structure this, either by naming the individual beneficiaries on the policy (the insurance company will then pay them directly), or by naming a charity as beneficiary on the RRSPs with the proceeds of the life insurance policy being paid to the estate. The concept is simple, but for optimal results it is recommended that an estate lawyer and financial planner familiar with estate planning be consulted.

1.5 Charitable bequest

Many elderly wish to leave something to a favorite charity. You certainly don't need to be a millionaire to leave a charitable bequest. If your parents are healthy, they can purchase a new policy to help achieve this goal. Alternatively, I often recommend that older policies that are no longer needed be used to leave a charitable bequest. A charitable bequest can be done in one of two ways:

- Name the charity in the will as beneficiary of the policy. This will provide tax relief in the year of death.

- Transfer ownership of the policy to a favorite charity, continue to pay the premiums, and collect a charitable tax credit each year the premium is paid.

1.6 The family cottage and balancing bequeathed assets

If your parent is in a position to leave one large asset (e.g., family cottage) to one child, while ensuring balance in what is bequeathed to other siblings, insurance can be a way to help achieve that desired financial balance.

Let's explore the home, family cottage, and Registered Retirement Savings Plan scenario by revisiting my client, Grace, and her daughters, Mary and Linda. Grace and I first met after her husband's death, and we talked about the need to update her will and powers of attorney (POAs). She had a clear idea that she wanted to leave half of her estate to each of her daughters. The assets included a family home valued at $250,000, a cottage with a current sale value of $150,000 and a cost base of $100,000, and an RRSP portfolio of $400,000.

Grace planned to leave both the house and the cottage to Mary, leave the RRSPs to Linda, and therefore leave each of her daughters with a $400,000 inheritance. What Grace neglected to take into account was the third silent beneficiary of her estate: Canada Revenue Agency (CRA)! This is completely understandable since when her husband had passed away, Grace inherited everything they owned on a tax-free basis thanks to spousal rollover. She neglected to take into account that the CRA has limits to its generosity and all taxes are due on the death of the second spouse. (The IRS in the US may act similarly.) Grace and I chatted about what would actually happen if she were to pursue her estate distribution as planned.

Grace's annual income is $45,000 from all sources, and in the previous year her combined federal and provincial taxes were approximately $7,200. If Grace were to pass away this year and her will stipulated that Mary was to receive both the house and the cottage, here is a quick snapshot of what would happen:

Grace's tax person would prepare a terminal return. Grace's income for the year would be as follows: $45,000 earned income plus $400,000 (from her RRSP) plus $50,000 in capital gains on the cottage (the appreciated value). The first thing the executor must do is to pay all debts. In this scenario, Grace's estate has a debt to the CRA and owes $197,264 in taxes ($124,059 in federal taxes plus $73,205 in provincial taxes).

The result? Mary receives the home and the cottage valued at $400,000. Linda receives the balance of the funds that used to be sheltered in Grace's RRSP ($400,000 minus taxes of $197,264) and now amounts to just $202,736. This is a far cry from treating each of her daughters equally, as she had intended.

In this situation, it is possible to restore Linda's share with the purchase of a life insurance policy for the amount owed to the CRA. Many elderly parents do exactly that. The other option is to revise the will to sell all assets and leave each child an equal amount of the remainder. Of course, in some families, the family home or cottage has great sentimental value to one or more of the children and the parents want it kept in the family.

Note the following in this case:

- The principal residence passes tax free.
- A cottage is deemed to be disposed (sold) and a claim must be made for the resulting capital gain.
- Registered Retirement Savings Plans, and other registered accounts such as Retirement Income Funds, Locked-In Retirement Accounts, and Locked-In Income Funds, are treated as income in the year of death and are fully taxable.
- In many cases, the taxes owing on an estate can exceed the estate's ability to create liquidity. This is where life insurance plays a vital role.

2. Types of Insurance

The following sections cover the different types of insurance.

2.1 Term life insurance

Term life insurance provides coverage at a fixed rate of payment for a limited period of time (the "term"). If the insured person dies during the term, the death benefit is paid (generally tax free) to the named beneficiary. After the term is over, another policy must be purchased at premiums which reflect current age and health. Needless to say, the new premiums will be substantially higher than the older policy. Term insurance is a good choice for young families on a budget who wish to protect their family from the financial loss of their death.

It is important that you find out if your parent already has an existing term insurance policy. He or she may have an older policy purchased years ago or a policy from a previous employer. If your parent is considering life insurance as part of his or her estate plans, it is important to act as soon as possible to see if it can be converted to a permanent policy. By reaching out to the related insurance agent, or company who issued the policy, you can find out if all, or part, of the policy can be converted. Often this is possible to do without a new medical examination. The timeliness is important, as term policies usually have an expiry date that the conversion must happen before, or it may expire when your parent reaches a certain age (e.g., 75 or 80).

2.2 Permanent insurance

Whole life and universal life (also known as "permanent") insurance is different from term life in that it guarantees coverage at fixed premiums for the lifetime of the covered individual. Similarly to term life, it pays a benefit on death to the named beneficiary, and that amount generally passes on tax free. If you are considering life insurance for some of the ideas presented in this chapter, you will need permanent life insurance.

Last-to-die policies are very popular with retirees, as the death benefit is paid out when it is needed, after the last death of the insured persons, your parents. The premiums are considerably less than insuring a single life, since the odds of both of your parents dying at the same time is less than the odds of one of them dying.

2.3 Long-term care insurance

The Canadian Life and Health Insurance Association Inc. (CLHIA) asserts that most Canadians mistakenly believe that the costs of living full time in a long-term care facility will be fully covered by government health-care programs. Unfortunately this not the case; only a small part of those costs may be covered, if at all. CLHIA statistics show that 74 percent of Canadians admit they have no financial plan to pay for long-term care if they need it. This is where long-term care insurance can be crucial (from http://clhia.uberflip.com/:/1199446; accessed January 20, 2014.)

Long-term care insurance provides financial protection for if and when your parent is not able to care for himself or herself any longer. It can cover the costs of stays in nursing homes or chronic care facilities, as well as the services of a caregiver in your parent's own home.

There are two different types of long-term care insurance plans. The first would reimburse your parent for eligible expenses that are outlined in whatever plan he or she chooses (e.g., private nursing services) up to a predetermined maximum. The second is an income-style plan that offers your parent a predetermined monthly (or daily or weekly) benefit amount, which you can spend any way you choose. Amounts could range from $20 to $400 per day, and the current monthly maximum is around $10,000.

Long-term care insurance can usually be bought up to age 80, and anyone who meets the insurance company's guidelines can buy it.

If you need help finding out which companies offer long-term care insurance, work with your financial planner or visit the United States Association of Insurance and Financial Advisors (NAIFA) at www.naifa.org. In Canada, you can contact the OmbudService for Life & Health Insurance at www.olhi.ca.

2.4 Critical illness insurance

Cancer, heart attack, and stroke are the most common critical illnesses that occur across all ages in North America. Recent numbers of people diagnosed with heart disease exceed 275,000[1] annually in Canada; cancer affects 185,000[2] and there are approximately 15,000 deaths due to stroke[3]. Americans can take little comfort in the US statistics; there were 14 million survivors of cardiovascular disease[4], 9.6 million cancer survivors[5], and it is expected 700,000 Americans will have a stroke[6] this year alone!

With all the advancements in medicine and treatments now available, the chances for recovery are better than ever. Treatments are expensive though, and not all of them are covered by government health plans. Recovery doesn't always mean you're back to your old self either. Often, after such diagnoses, patients require medical and physical support once they're back home, which can be costly.

Critical illness insurance plans pay you a cash lump sum, 30 days after diagnosis, if you are diagnosed with a life-threatening illness such as cancer, heart disease (requiring surgery), heart attack, or stroke. Some critical illness policies cover many other illnesses such as organ transplants, blindness, dementia, Alzheimer's disease, and beyond. Critical illness insurance can be bought with guaranteed

---

1 www.heartandstroke.com/site/c.iklQLcMWJtE/b.3483991/K.34A8/Statistics.htm, accessed January 29, 2014.

2 www.cancer.ca/en/cancer-information/cancer-101/cancer-statistics-at-a-glance/?region-on, accessed January 29, 2014.

3 www.strokecenter.org/patients/about-stroke/stroke-statistics, accessed January 29, 2014.

4 www.cdc.gov, accessed January 29, 2014

5 www.cdc.gov, accessed January 29, 2014

6 www.cdc.gov, accessed January 29, 2014

(fixed) premiums that won't go up over the years, helping you and your parents budget consistently and well in advance.

One of the top benefits to critical illness insurance is the ability to use that lump-sum payment any way you want. You can use it for medical equipment or services, or you can pay off existing debt you have, or you can take that once in a lifetime trip with your family you always dreamed of. It's totally up to you. Another great thing? It's tax free!

This type of insurance can usually be purchased up to age 65, and is generally sold in amounts ranging between $10,000 and $2,000,000. Some policies offer long-term care insurance built in to their critical illness insurance so it's important to get those details and avoid buying two separate policies if you don't need to do so. Be aware that once a claim has been paid, the coverage typically terminates.

In some instances, the policy is purchased by, and premiums paid by, the adult child. This is particularly true where the beneficiary will be the adult child. The policy can help the child be ready to help his or her parents deal with the challenges they will face if and when their health declines, and be prepared with the financial solutions to help them choose the best option for them if they need to transition to a lifestyle that involves in-home support or the move to a retirement home or care facility.

Chapter 9 will help you identify when the moment has arrived to help parents transition to assisted living, and how to best approach it with your parent.

Helping Aging Parents Transition to a Life of Increased Dependence

Building on much of the information we discussed about caregiving in Chapter 1, it's time to get into more detail on the care and facility options involved when your parents can no longer live independently in their own home, as well as how to help them transition to a new home. This chapter is organized to take you through the stages your parents are likely to face as they progress from a life of full independence, to needing help, to dependence, and finally, end-of-life care.

1. When Is It Time to Get Help?

The first step is to know when it is time for your parents to get help. I have dealt with many people over the years (my own siblings included) that were simply unable or unwilling to acknowledge when their parents' health was failing. Many of us have trouble admitting our parents are human, and it is not easy to face the fact that they won't be around forever. This is an emotional time. Each person deals with this situation differently, in his or her own way and at his or her own speed. I have seen many siblings argue over whether or not their parents need help, which is challenging for everyone involved. The most important piece of advice I can give you is to eliminate the emotional component as much as possible by seeking outside help and advice from friends and medical professionals who are removed from the situation and can be objective.

It may be you who is having difficulty accepting it is time for help; it could be your sibling, or another family member. The following sections will provide you with some of the signs that help is likely required for your parents.

1.1 Signs your parents need help

In Chapter 1 we discussed some tips on bow to be a detective and look for evidence of difficulty when you visit your parents' home. We also discussed the activities of daily living: continence (going to the bathroom on their own), bathing, getting in and out of bed, dressing, and feeding. Obviously, if any of these activities are presenting a challenge for your parents, you know they need help immediately.

If you need to, check with friends of your parents or their neighbors to get more information or if you're unsure about the conclusions you're drawing. Often, people may have insights that they were reluctant to share for fear of appearing nosy or overstepping boundaries.

The following list is some of the many things you should be concerned about if you notice them about a parent:

1. Your parent has just experienced the onset of a chronic illness (e.g., heart disease, arthritis, or diabetes).

2. Your parent has just lost his or her driver's license. The authorities don't take a person's driver's license away without good reason. Accept that this is symptomatic of a legitimate issue and dig deeper to find out why.

3. Your parent has experienced getting lost recently, or forgetting the names of family members, children, or grandchildren.

4. You notice that there is a shortage of food in your parent's house; perhaps an empty fridge or cupboards.

5. Your parent's level of personal hygiene has declined from what they usually maintained in the past.

6. You notice your parent is having increased difficulty with banking and understanding finances or has recently been taken advantage of financially.

7. Your parent is withdrawing socially. He or she no longer participates in activities that he or she used to, and might even be approaching a shut-in lifestyle.

8. Your parent has experienced a recent fall and possibly broke a hip or suffered another injury as a result.

Once you've identified an issue, it's time to alert other family members and agree on the best way to move forward. Acting alone, before asking for input from other people who love your parents (e.g., siblings) can cause conflict. Voice your concerns and base them on evidence rather than emotion. Explain what you've seen and how you have learned that these are signs it is time to step in and help. If you still experience resistance from other family members, you can explore steps we discussed in earlier chapters, such as partnering with your parents' physician to help you.

When you're ready to approach your parents to talk about how to best support them during this challenging time, remember how hard it will be for them to acknowledge they are facing a loss of their independence and control. It will be difficult for them to accept their increasing frailty and they will likely be frustrated by the things they can no longer do for themselves. Be aware that you may be fighting an uphill battle for a while in helping them see that they do need help.

Try to explain things in a positive way. For example, say your mom needs to give up her license because her driving is no longer safe. You and your siblings could approach the subject by saying, "We will be your personal chauffeurs!" Another example; assume your dad hates cooking, but he loves dessert. Explain that if he moves into a home, all the cooking will be done for him and every meal will come with a choice of dessert (this may vary depending on the care home). A bonus is that he'll never have to wash dishes again! Helping your parent write out a list of positive benefits (avoid negatives) of whatever changes are necessary will help make the transition easier.

1.2 I'm not ready yet

If your parents aren't ready to accept that they need help, you're in good company. Senior housing professionals will tell you that they often hear first-time visitors say "I'm not ready yet!" However, once people make the decision to move to a retirement community, those same people often declare "What was I waiting for?"

If you think you may have difficulty convincing your parents that it's time to get help, try approaching the conversation with a series of questions that will help them realize their growing limitations. Try any or all of the questions in Worksheet 9 as a starting point toward building their self-awareness. (This worksheet is included in the download kit so you can print it and write down their answers.)

As I mentioned in an earlier chapter, one of the books I find most helpful in this regard is *How to Say It to Seniors: Closing the Communication Gap with Our Elders* by David Solie. I learned from Solie's book that the elderly do not deal well with unsolicited advice, so be careful how much you offer during this process. Asking questions is usually a far more effective approach than offering advice. Solie's book shows that seniors have unique communication needs related to language, phrases, and vocabulary. They also have very different agendas than those of us with fewer years under our belts. Understanding those needs and agendas can truly minimize frustration for everyone involved. Appreciating the need seniors have for control (something that they are losing more of with each passing year), and their desire to have a legacy and be remembered, are just a couple of the ways you can tailor your conversations to be more effective.

Once you and your parents identify there are needs, position your ideas as helpful suggestions to help them *retain* their independence. For example, if they are reaching the point where they simply can't cook for themselves any longer, suggest having Meals on Wheels deliver so they can keep their independence and live at home longer. The earlier you start getting them assistance, the easier the transition to full-time care will be later on. Building in a little help in stages over time is far easier to digest than suddenly going from complete independence to selling their home, leaving everything behind, and moving to a retirement home.

The elderly may feel they are losing control, so anything you can do to give them independence will make things more comfortable

Worksheet 9
Building Your Parents' Self-Awareness That They Need Help

1. Do you ever suffer from loneliness?

2. Has your social life become restricted lately?

3. Do you find you feel less safe in your home than you used to?

4. Do you wish you could get more exercise?

5. Is home maintenance (e.g., gardening) becoming more of a burden than a joy?

6. Do you avoid driving at night?

7. Since you lost your driver's license, are you having difficulty getting out for appointments, shopping, and socializing?

8. Are housekeeping chores more difficult than they used to be?

9. Is caring for an ill spouse becoming too challenging to manage?

10. Have your eating habits changed?

11. Are you eating alone too often?

12. Do you worry about who will respond in case of emergency?

13. Is your health declining?

14. Have you mixed up or forgotten any of your medications?

15. Would you be more comfortable if you had some supportive services to assist you?

for them. For example, giving the person a choice gives him or her independence because he or she has some control over the situation. Even a simple choice such as "Would you like Betty or Joe to drive you to the doctor's office?" will encourage the person to take part in the decision making for his or her own well-being.

2. Preparing for the Move

There are many options available to support your parents through the variety of stages of dependence they will be going through as they age. In addition to evaluating cost and what they can afford, I want to remind you to consider the equal importance of location. Most seniors do not like to move. They want to stay close to what they are familiar with such as shops, professional services (e.g., doctor, dentist), community centers, religious centers, and friends. They may also have language barriers that would make moving to a new community that much more difficult. Keep these factors in mind when considering the location of any options that involve moving from their current home. Ensuring they stay close to what they know, or at least find a new location that shares many of the same attributes, or one where existing friends are already living, will make a move much easier to deal with.

Before you help your parent make a move, keep the following information in mind to help them feel at home in their new surroundings.

2.1 Choose wisely to reduce stress

Before making a final decision on a new place, ask your parent if he or she is happy with the location. Many elderly prefer to stay in a familiar neighborhood, even if it is far from family members.

Are the doors wide enough to accommodate a wheelchair? Even if your parent does not use a wheelchair now, he or she may need one in the future, and moving again would be very stressful. Look for walk-in or, even better, wheel-in closets.

Are the windows large and do they offer a view? How is the heating and air conditioning? Many elderly people, as their metabolisms slow, suffer from being too cold. Spend at least 30 minutes in the room with your family member to see how comfortable he or she is. How far away is the dining room? Can he or she get there on his or her own?

2.2 Reduce furniture

Your family member has likely been living in the same home for many years. Current furniture may be too plentiful or too large. Use a floor plan of the new space and use cut-outs scaled to the size of the furniture you are thinking of bringing to the new accommodations. In order to make getting around easier, don't forget to leave room for walkers and wheelchairs.

2.3 Think about storage

Try to estimate how much shelving will be needed. As parents age, it is much easier to use an open shelf to store clothing than a drawer that has to be opened. Drawers can be heavy and stiff, reducing your loved one's independence if he or she has to call for help to get a sweater. Don't forget to make room for all those family pictures and memorabilia. Install additional shelving as needed.

2.4 Consider safety and convenience

For safety's sake, conceal electrical wiring along baseboards wherever possible. Loose wires can cause falls. Provide remote controls for items such as windows, televisions, and lights. Making these items easier to use helps the elderly maintain independence. Not sure if the new accommodations are safe enough? Call your local seniors' service provider and request a safety assessment.

2.5 Prepare to say goodbye to many things

When downsizing to an apartment, retirement home, or long-term care facility, there will be little need or room for things such as cleaning supplies, laundry items, pantry items, pots, pans, dinnerware, glasses, and crystal. Bedding and towels can be reduced, or eliminated if they are being provided by the home. Your elderly family member may wish to keep a few favorite items to remind him or her of home.

Because many elderly are attached to their possessions, you may find it easier to suggest items be given to a family member who could use or might want the things being discarded. Perhaps a grandchild who is just starting out on his or her own could use a set of dishes, pots, and pans. Make suggestions such as, "Mom, your cool wardrobe from the 1960s might look cute on your granddaughter, don't you think? She loves to shop at all the vintage stores. Wouldn't it be a nice memory for both of you?"

2.6 Show respect for your parent's opinions and feelings

Your parent has opinions. After all, this is going to be his or her new home and you want him or her to feel at home as soon as possible. The best way to do this is to provide as many familiar possessions as possible. You may hate that old recliner with the duct tape on the armrest, but suck it up! This is not about good taste, or you! Ask your loved one to make a list of "must have" possessions, and try to accommodate. If you have to buy new items to fit, involve your loved one in the purchase-making decisions. The more it looks like home, the easier the emotional transition will be, and the less traumatic the adjustment.

2.7 Have valuables appraised

When going through your parent's possessions keep your eyes open for items they will not be bringing with them which may be of value. If your parents have collections of art, antiques, or a complete set of comic books, it is a good idea to hire an appraiser who can help you to place a realistic selling price on these items. Who knows, you may uncover the complete original set of 1964 Barbie and Ken wedding party set dolls in mint condition, currently valued at $2,600! It is one of the responsibilities of the power of attorney to ensure that valuables are properly valued and the best sale price is achieved.

3. Moving to a Smaller Home

Downsizing to a smaller home, a condo, or an apartment may be the right step for your parent if the main challenge he or she faces is keeping up with housekeeping and home maintenance. Condos and apartments typically include services for shoveling snow, mowing the lawn, and minor in-suite repairs to plumbing and electrical. They may have elevators from the parking garage right to your parent's floor that can help with minor accessibility challenges as well. Many buildings have social committees that plan events to keep residents connected and social, a great added value if your loved one's social life has been in decline.

Before deciding to purchase a smaller home or condo, consider how long your parent will be able to live independently. If it is less than five years, I would suggest that buying is not the right choice. I believe the elderly are better served by renting. If your parent is considering purchasing a smaller home or condo to increase his or her retirement income, the difference between the selling price of the existing home and the purchase price of the new home needs to be large enough to provide the additional income needed. Consider that a net gain of $100,000 will provide approximately $10,000 a year for ten years. Do not forget to take into account the various costs of both selling and purchasing (i.e., realtor fees, land transfer tax, moving costs, decorating the new home). If downsizing is the right option for your parent at this time, be sure to read Chapter 10 for more details on selling his or her current home.

3.1 Granny suites

A granny suite is a self-contained unit that is attached to an existing home and has its own full kitchen, bath facilities, and a separate entrance. Sometimes it is referred to as an in-law suite. A granny suite can also be a separate living unit that is not attached to an existing home, but is built on the same property; this is often referred to as a garden suite.

Canada Mortgage and Housing Corporation (CMHC) offers financial assistance for the development of either of these granny suites when it is being created for a low-income senior in Canada. You do not need to be related to the senior involved. As long as your property meets the applicable zoning and building requirements, you can apply for eligibility with CMHC. The assistance is in the form of a forgivable loan that does not have to be repaid, provided that you (the owner) adhere to the conditions of the program. The loan ranges from $24,000 to $36,000 depending on where, in Canada, you live. You can consider creating this option for your parent on your own property (or that of another relative), or you can seek rental properties that others have developed. These are often affordable alternatives to the seniors staying in their own, larger homes, and offer them the potential to stay within their own community.

4. United States Subsidized Housing for Seniors

American readers will find access to subsidized rental apartments through the U.S. Department of Housing and Urban Development (HUD). The applicants must be at least 62 years old and meet HUD's definition of low income, typically meaning the person's income is 50 percent or less than the area's regional median income. For more information go to www.hud.gov.

In addition to federal rental assistance programs, there may be programs offered by your state or regional government. Churches and charities often offer programs for housing for low-income elderly.

5. Canadian Rent Geared to Income

Rent geared to income is a program offered by Canada's regional governments to provide affordable housing options for qualified seniors. Rent is determined as a percentage of the senior's total taxable income (e.g., 25 percent). There are buildings designated for this purpose, and lengthy waiting lists are often involved so it is best to apply early. Those with special priority status, health and safety priority status, or homeless status may be given higher priority. The elderly person may qualify for special priority if a case can be made for the safety of his or her current living arrangements. In order to qualify, the senior must be able to demonstrate an ability to live independently, even if it is with the assistance of aids (e.g., walkers, wheelchairs) or home care.

6. Home Care

If your parents are just starting to need personal care at home and they can get by with occasional help with housekeeping, personal support for hygiene, and routine personal activities (e.g., eating, dressing, escorting to appointments) then Canadians can reach out to the Community Care Access Centre (CCAC) to help determine parents' specific needs and find out about available financial subsidies. If your parent is eligible (determined by the CCAC), the services arranged can be paid for by the Ministry of Health and long-term care. Otherwise, you will be responsible for the fees involved, but the CCAC can still help you source needed services.

In the United States, providers of home care are predominately offered by the private sector. This type of care is called "formal home care" as opposed to "informal care" provided by a family member. Nurse Next Door is an example of a franchise dedicated to home care for the elderly.

As your parents' health and strength declines, you will find they need more help. Once your parents are in need of supervised care, in other words when it is no longer safe for them to live alone, you, as their caregiver, will have to consider the options available to you. One option is for them to continue to live at home with a family member, with or without the help of private home-care professionals.

Private home-care services can range from $5 to $30 per hour (or more) for in-home meal preparation, and homemaking. Personal care for bathing, dressing, and other activities of daily living when provided by a trained, nonmedical professional can range from $15 to $40 per hour. The cost of services for professional nursing care are the most expensive, you can expect the hourly rate to range from $25 to $85 per hour. The variance in costs is largely determined by where you live. Smaller communities can be expected to have lower costs than large metropolitan areas.

The costs of in-home care can rise quickly, especially once your parent requires 24-hour care. A full-time, live-in personal-care worker can cost $1,800 to $3,000 a month, plus room and board.[1] Add another

---

1 "The toughest choice," *MoneySense*, accessed January 20, 2014. www.moneysense.ca/retire/the-toughest-choice-2

$1,500 to $2,000 if room and board are not provided. If your parent needs around-the-clock care that may require two or three full-time caregivers since they can each only be asked to work one shift per day, and they require time off. Don't forget that those new costs will be in addition to the existing costs of running your parent's home (e.g., property tax, cable, electricity). On top of all that, additional renovations may also be required for ramps instead of stairs, more accessible bathtubs, and wheelchair accessibility upgrades.

As the adult child, you will be required to hire and manage staff, provide scheduling, deal with your elderly parent's complaints, and possibly fire a caregiver who proves to be unsatisfactory. All of this takes time, and adds to the stress of caring for your elderly parent. It's hard to put a dollar value on what "stress" is worth to the average person, but trust me from personal experience, it's costly!

7. Retirement Residences

Retirement residences come in many shapes and sizes. They can be totally independent living accommodations that are built-in communities that offer the organization of social events and activities to people of a certain age group. Accommodations may be private studios, or one- or two-bedroom apartments. Seniors are surrounded by other people of a similar age, who likely have a lot in common and wish to live somewhere with a sense of community.

Retirement residences can also offer more than that, such as allowing for independent living while also providing one to three meals a day, along with conveniences such as laundry services on the same floor, for example. Residents are still independent enough to manage their own medications, and perform most or all of the activities of daily living. This level of accommodation is great for those who can still care for themselves but who find shopping and housekeeping use up too much of their energy and leave little for socializing and fun.

When I first started looking for retirement homes for my parents, I was looking at fully independent homes where the chores of living at home would be eliminated. Mom waited too long though, and is now in the assisted living building (right next door to the independent living building owned and operated by the same company).

Assisted-living residences offer more support to individuals or couples who need housekeeping, meals, assistance with their personal care, and the availability of staff on a 24-hour basis. Residents may need help with bathing, mobility, or taking their medications. Assisted living is for those who are having difficulty performing one or more Activities of Daily Living. The residents in assisted-living accommodations require supervised care, so there is a higher staff-to-resident ratio. As your parents' capabilities diminish they may be advised to move to a long-term care facility. The waiting lists for long-term care homes can be very long so it is good idea to have your parent's name placed on a waiting list.

Independent and assisted-living residences are not funded by the government, but are owned and managed by private corporations (some may be nonprofit). You will not need to provide medical evidence that your parent needs care; the home will assess your parent's needs to ensure they are able to properly care for them.

Short-term stays (respite) are also usually available at these facilities and might be a helpful option for your parent if he or she is still being cared for at home and you, as the primary caregiver, need a break. Respite stays are a way for your elderly parent to take a "test drive" to see how he or she fits in, and it provides the staff with the opportunity to see if they can meet your parent's needs. From my personal experience, my mother wanted to go to the independent living building, but once there, the staff alerted us to her constant needs, which required her moving to the assisted-living building. Though she resisted at first, after a few weeks she welcomed the increased staff ratio and the fact that she could ring her buzzer for help as much as needed.

Residence fees may seem high at first glance, but it is important to take into account all the bells and whistles that are included in that fee. While your parents would likely need a vehicle if they were living at home, a retirement residence typically provides shuttle bus service for trips to the mall or social outings — that means no more gas, insurance, or maintenance costs (e.g., tires and oil changes). At home, your parents are responsible for their utility bills, property tax, cable and telephone bills, which add up to hundreds of dollars every month. At a retirement residence, all those items are usually included. There is no need for housekeeping, lawn care, or snow removal at a retirement residence either, so your parents won't need to pay for those services now that it is too physically demanding for them to handle on their own.

When you're visiting retirement residences, be sure to ask about additional fees. Some residences charge for services (e.g., bathing, supervision, and dispensing medicines). Costs can range from $500 per month to more than $5,000. Some homes charge for "time," others charge by the additional "service" provided. An example of a time charge is how my mother's residence charges $500 per month for every hour of daily private assistance above the allotted base line provided to all residents. An example of a service charge is where a resident might be charged for the dispensing and supervision of medications or for help with bathing.

My client, Grace, is living comfortably in an assisted-living retirement home for $2,800 per month, and based on her savings she can live there indefinitely without worrying about running out of money. This would not be the case if she were faced with the costs of 24-hour supervised care in her own home.

In case your parent needs reminding, here are some of the top benefits of retirement living:

- Allows independent living for a longer period of time, with the privacy, choice, and freedom you value so dearly.
- Your parent's level of physical nourishment will likely improve, as the meals provided are well-balanced.
- Your parent's level of social activity will likely increase thanks to having someone else organize and facilitate those activities, along with arranging for transportation.
- The timeliness of the support required will be very good, with professionals available to help with medications, health questions, and administrative tasks.
- No more household chores. What a pleasure!
- The convenience of the location of many of these residences is very high, with locations chosen in close proximity to shopping, restaurants, and other amenities.
- Companionship is often better as well, with other retired neighbors for socializing.
- Stress levels are reduced thanks to ample support, fewer chores, better security, and a sense of community.

8. Long-Term Care Facilities

Long-term care (LTC) facilities are different from retirement homes in that they provide assistance with the Activities of Daily Living and offer 24-hour nursing care and much higher levels of personal care. They are also known as nursing homes. LTC facilities can be owned by private corporations, nonprofit organizations, or municipal governments.

LTC facilities can accommodate a wider range of health needs with onsite supervision and increased personal safety levels. LTC costs can range from $900 to more than $5,000 per month depending on the room type (e.g., single or shared), the services and amenities, and the level of government funding available. In Canada, residents of long-term care facilities pay for their own accommodation costs (i.e., rent) while the cost of nursing and personal care is covered by the provincial government. If your parent is low income, he or she may qualify for a rate reduction on the rental costs.

Short-term stays (respites) are also usually available at long-term care facilities, and might be a helpful option for your parents if they are still being cared for at home, and you are their primary caregiver and need to take a break.

When thinking of the costs involved, especially when comparing to those of living at home, you may find Worksheet 10 helpful in seeing which option is truly more expensive. In many cases, the cost difference can be quite negligible. (The download kit includes this form for your use.)

9. Palliative Care

Palliative care is the area of health care that focuses on relieving pain and suffering for patients who are dealing with illness, thereby improving their quality of life. A palliative care facility will involve a multidisciplinary approach to caring for your ailing parent, using input from doctors, nurses, social workers, psychologists, religious personnel, and others. The main goal is to minimize suffering in the patient's life, as he or she is fighting a terminal illness with life expectancy of (usually) three months or less (the usual amount of time one is expected to live at a hospice).

Palliative medicine focuses on relieving symptoms, rather than curing the disease or cause. For example, if your parent is dealing with cancer, he or she would be treated for the nausea that might accompany chemotherapy, and given any emotional, spiritual, or other support that he or she would find helpful. At a hospice, this support is usually extended to family members as well, helping them deal with the loss and grief that takes place during the illness of their loved one and bereavement.

Worksheet 10
Living at Home versus Retirement Residence

Living at Home versus Retirement Residence

Expenses	My Monthly Costs	Retirement Home	Expenses	My Monthly Costs	Retirement Home
Food			**Discretionary Expenses**		
Housing			Fitness/Physio/Massage		
Mortgage/Rent			Travel/Vacation		
Utilities (e.g., heat, electricity)			Hobbies		
Phone/Cell/Internet			Pets		
Home Insurance			Entertainment		
Property Tax			Subscriptions		
Condominium Fees			**Health Care**		
Maintenance			Eye/Dental		
Housekeeping			Prescriptions		
Lawn/Snow Removal			Home Care		
Transportation			Respite		
Taxis			Other		
Public Transportation					
Daily Living					
Clothing					
Grooming/Personal Care					
Subtotal	0	0	**Subtotal**	0	0
Total					

10. Do Your Homework

Before choosing any new accommodations for your parent, be sure to do your homework. Arrange for an initial tour of the facility to meet with those who run it and find out pricing and service information. Once you have created a shortlist of facilities that meet your parent's needs for health, safety, location, and lifestyle, revisit each of the final options to do a more thorough inspection of areas such as washrooms, common areas, kitchens, and laundry facilities. Look for high levels of cleanliness and hygiene. Ask to speak with current residents to get their feedback. Look for articles in local papers or on the Internet that offer more information in the form of reviews or information.

You can use Worksheet 11 when comparing retirement residences to evaluate all the factors aside from cost (e.g., amenities, services, location). You and your parent may find this helpful in making a final decision between different options that they can afford. You can print a copy of this worksheet from the download kit.

With the proper research and preparation, you can help your aging parents find the best living accommodations for each stage of their life, keeping them safe, healthy, and happy in their later years!

Comparing Retirement Homes

Features	Residence 1		Residence 2		Residence 3	
	Yes	No	Yes	No	Yes	No
Safety and Cleanliness						
24-hour security						
Reception desk to screen visitors/phone calls						
Air-conditioned building						
Air-conditioned resident rooms						
Fire alarms						
Cleanliness of kitchen						
Cleanliness of utility, storage, and garbage areas						
Health-Care Services						
Doctor						
Doctor on staff						
Doctor on call						
In-house scheduled doctor visits						
Option to retain family doctor						
Nursing						
24-hour nursing staff						
Credentials of other caregivers						
Option to retain additional outside caregivers						
Coordination with other services						

Medical services								
Supervised medication								
Medications administered by staff								
Access to medical services								
Visiting dentist								
Visiting audiologist								
Visiting optometrist								
Podiatry services								
Massage therapy services								
Chiropractor services								
Physiotherapy services								
Laboratory onsite								
Pharmacy onsite								
Available Services								
Housekeeping								
Laundry: linens and towels								
Laundry: personal items								
Recreation program								
Fitness program								
Dining								
Meals included (e.g., all three meals, or only lunch and supper)								
Quality of meals (i.e., healthy choices)								

Worksheet 11 — Continued

Choice of menu															
Accommodation for special dietary needs (e.g., allergy restrictions)															
Comfortable dining area															
Refreshments or snacks offered between meals															
Dietician or Nutritionist on staff															
Transportation															
Group outings															
Personal appointments															
Parking for residents															
Parking for visitors															
Amenities															
Garden															
Chapel															
Hair salon															
Theater															
Library															
Recreation/Game room															
Computer room															
ATM for personal banking															
Respite suites															
Guest suites															

Utilities Included										
Electricity										
Heat										
Water										
Telephone										
Cable										
Internet										
Accommodations										
Studio suite										
One-bedroom suite										
Two-bedroom suite										
Roomy										
Well laid-out floor plan										
Kitchenette in suite (e.g., includes bar fridge and/or microwave)										
Pleasant view from windows										
Patio/Balcony										
Curtains or blinds included										
Wheelchair accessible										
Bathtub										
Shower										

Adequate storage space (e.g., shelves, closets, counter space)			
Secure access (e.g., lock and/or peephole)			
Emergency call system			
Fire alarm/sprinkler system in suites			
Convenient electrical outlets			
Individual control for heating and air conditioning in suite			
Pricing			
Base cost	$	$	$
Extra services	$	$	$
Additional costs	$	$	$
Overall Satisfaction Rating			

Selling the Family Home

When your parents are ready to leave the family home, your work begins to ensure they receive the best price possible when they sell. Don't get distracted by the emotional nature of this in the process, as tough as it may be on your parents, yourself, and any siblings you may have. Many good memories were likely created in that home, and it's natural to get emotional when thinking of it changing hands. Keep your eye on the ball, though! You want to add as much to their retirement savings as possible with this valuable asset, so leave emotions aside as much as you can. At this point, it is safe to say that your parents require your help either due to loss of health, mental capacity, or both.

1. Step 1: Prepare

The first step is to look into who has the authority to sell the home, sign the realtor's contract, and sign the offer of sale. If you are not your parent's power of attorney for property, you will need to obtain approval, in writing, in advance of hiring an agent and accepting an offer of sale.

During this process, if your parents are still currently living at home, it is worth considering moving them to their next destination or retirement residence *before* you sell. This may seem like jumping the gun, but I have a good reason for making this recommendation. It can be very difficult for the elderly to witness the sale of their beloved home, not to mention prepare for showings, pack their belongings, select what they will keep and what must be disposed of or given away, and to participate in this emotional process. Facilitating the move before the many tasks involved with the sale of the home can help you avoid everything happening all at once, along with the emotional components being layered on as well.

2. Step 2: Select a Realtor

The next step is to select and hire a realtor to sell your parents' home. When hiring a realtor, I recommend that three agents, from three different firms be interviewed before you make a final selection. That may seem like extra work at a point in your life when you likely don't have much time to spare, but I truly believe it is worth the effort.

Finding the right person to maximize the sale price of your parents' home can provide tens of thousands of additional dollars for their nest egg. That amount of money can go a long way, especially over a period of years when it is invested well and can still grow. Try your best not to rush this process and you won't be sorry.

Here is what you are looking for when seeking the right realtor:

- An experienced realtor who has at least seven years of experience in the real estate business servicing the local area.
- Someone who is hard working with a proven history of sales, and who is available and accessible at all times.
- Someone who is articulate and a great communicator, with the ability to negotiate in your best interests. You want an aggressive negotiator, not someone out to make a quick sale at your expense.
- Someone who is honest, even blunt, and will tell you the "real deal" on how salable the home is, and what needs to be done to maximize the sale price.

- Someone who is a good networker. This is a people business. Some homes sell because agents have connections with other agents.

The candidates should provide you with a suggested sale price that is realistic, according to the comparable homes sold in that neighborhood within the last six months. The home should be priced to sell within 30 days. Any longer than that and momentum gets lost as the listing becomes stale. You don't want to be forced to deal with a price reduction.

Commission charged can vary from one realtor to the next, and in many cases can be a function of their marketing plan. Some agents will agree up front to offer a rebate in commission if they represent both the buyer and the seller in the transaction. Doing so can save you thousands of dollars so be sure to ask about this scenario. Though commission rate is important, remember to keep all factors in mind when choosing the realtor. The lowest cost may not be the best value, especially if the realtor isn't able to sell the home for the best price.

The most important element a realtor brings to the sale process is his or her marketing plan. This is where you need to do the most research by asking questions. A solid marketing plan is more important than the suggested sale price and commission the realtor will charge. It's crucial.

What you want to know in terms of the realtor's marketing plan is how he or she will meet the following expectations:

1. Professional signage, including the agent's cell phone number.
2. Lockbox for showings.
3. Daily electronic monitoring of lockbox access.
4. Follow-up reports on buyer showings and feedback from prospective buyers.
5. Broker previews.
6. Incentives for broker or office previews.
7. Staging advice (and potentially covering the partial or full cost of staging)
8. Weekly advertising in major newspapers.
9. Advertising in local newspapers.

10. MLS exposure with 8 to 12 professional photographs.

11. Virtual online tour.

12. Distribution to major websites.

13. Four-color flyers.

14. Financing flyers for potential buyers.

15. Minimum of two open houses, providing its location is a candidate.

16. Direct-mail to surrounding neighbors, out-of-area buyers, and brokers.

17. Exposure at board of realtor meetings.

18. Feedback to sellers on buyer sign calls and buyer showings.

19. Email feeds of new listings that compete.

20. Updates on neighborhood facts, trends, and recent sales.

You can use Worksheet 12 during the process of interviewing potential realtors. This will help you record responses and have a basis for comparison before making a final decision. You can print this worksheet from the download kit.

Even if your parents are going to stay in the home during the sale process, as the realtor will likely tell you, it will help the sale (both in speed and price) to remove as much clutter and as many personal knickknacks as possible before listing the home. As hard as it may be to remove and pack those things, prospective buyers want to imagine themselves living there, and that is hard to do when they are seeing personal photos and memorabilia from another family all over the house. Help them visualize the clean slate they're looking for by removing clutter and personal items. This will also make it much easier to keep the home clean and ready for viewing when prospective buyers want to see it.

Leave the rest to the professionals. That's why you're paying a commission to the agent. He or she is there to help facilitate the sale and handle all the negotiating, marketing, and paperwork. Once you've done the work in selecting the right agent, take a break and let him or her handle the rest. Save your energy for when it's time to pack all those boxes!

Worksheet 12
Questions to Ask a Realtor

Question	Agent 1	Agent 2	Agent 3
How long have you been a realtor in this area?			
As an agent, what geographic area do you most often represent?			
What is the average sale price of your completed transactions? Do you normally sell in this price range?			
Please provide a copy of your marketing plan for this home.			
What price range do you expect for this home? How realistic is this price?			
How did you arrive at this price or price range?			
What homes, if any, have sold in this area in the past six months? Can you provide supporting data (five or more)? *(You want to see comparables for at least a ten-block radius.)*			
How much was the final selling price for those listings?			
What, if anything, can we do to enhance the salability of this home?			

How much would you recommend we spend to increase the value of this home?			
What would the payback be if we went ahead with the changes?			
What is the length of time it will take to sell this home?			
When is the best time to list?			
What is the commission you charge?			
Will you reduce your commission if you or your firm represents both the seller and buyer of this home?			
In the event our relationship is unsatisfactory, can we cancel our contract with you?			

chapter 11

Succeed with Good Advice

Integrity is choosing your thoughts and actions based on values rather than personal gain.

— Anonymous

There are many professionals who can assist you with great advice and experience as you go through the process outlined in this book.

You may already be happy with your parents' current advisors. If that's the case, that is great news! The continuity and familiarity they'll enjoy in dealing with people they already know will be very helpful during this challenging time.

If you have doubts about your current advisors, if you're not sure if they are performing as well as they could be, or you do not yet have any advisors at all, then this chapter is for you!

The key is to *identify* and select a team of professionals you *trust*. How do you know who you can trust? In this chapter I will provide you with the tools to interview, select, and hire the right people to help you as you assume responsibility for the caregiving of your elderly parents. Bonus points go to prospective advisors who have their Certified Professional Consultant on Aging (CPCA) designation, as they have therefore demonstrated an interest in working with the elderly, and it's likely because a good percentage of their clients already fit into this demographic (another bonus).

I highly recommend you make the effort to become familiar with the professionals who can help you to achieve your goals. Hire the advisors you feel comfortable with and on whose advice you can rely. A good advisor is always willing to admit where his or her area of expertise ends and is willing to seek the advice of the other professionals as required.

The key professional relationships you will need in your journey as caregiver are discussed in the following sections.

1. Accountant

You'll need an accountant (or equivalent) who will be responsible for preparing tax returns. The ideal candidate will be able to offer proactive advice throughout the year to ensure you do not miss any tax-saving opportunities. It is a good idea to seek a tax planner who is already working with the elderly. Not only will he or she be better informed on tax issues and credits available to the elderly, he or she will likely demonstrate a greater emotional connection, along with the patience required to work with the elderly and their overworked caregivers.

2. Lawyer

You will need the advice of a dedicated estate lawyer to complete the power of attorney and will documents. Many lawyers run a general practice, offering services in many areas. Their specialty may be real estate, for example, and while they may be willing and able to write a simple will and power of attorney, you should wonder how good they are going to be if estate law makes up only a small percentage of their day-to-day practice.

3. Financial Planner

Because there are so many designations, ways to work, and differences in costs, the world of financial planning can be confusing. Many advisors call themselves "financial planners" when, in fact, they should call themselves either "investment advisors" or an "insurance advisors." Generally, an advisor is one who gives "advice" on a specific or particular area of finances, and is compensated for doing so. This compensation is usually with commissions at the time the client makes a purchase of whatever product (e.g., insurance, mutual fund, stocks, bonds) the advisor sells.

A "planner" may give the same advice, and be paid in the same way, but the difference is that a planner provides advice beyond the scope of the product being sold. Anyone who calls himself or herself a financial planner should provide an actual "plan." The plan should include action items such as the following:

- How to achieve a set of goals as outlined by the client.
- Advice for minimizing taxation.
- How much and what kind of insurance to buy.
- How much money needs to be saved, at what rate of return, and for how long.

If you are looking for a planner, one of the very best credentials available is the Certified Financial Planner (CFP). The Certified Financial Planner designation is recognized internationally as the mark of a competent, ethical, and professional financial planner. CFPs are found in all areas of financial services. They may work for banks, credit unions, insurance companies, investment firms, accounting firms, full-service financial planning firms, stock brokerage firms, or in their own private practice.

CFPs who work in the banking, insurance, or investment industry may prepare a full financial plan at no direct expense to you, since the commission from the sale of products you buy pays for this service. Some CFPs work on an hourly or fee-for-service basis. These professionals do not sell products but rather are paid for their time. Be sure to ask how your planner is paid and how much it will cost you.

You will find a list of all CFPs in good standing in the US by contacting the Certified Financial Planner Board of Standards (www.cfp.net); in Canada, you can contact the Financial Planning Standards Council (www.fpsc.ca/directory-cfp-professionals-good-standing).

3.1 The benefits of working with a financial planner

As a financial planner myself, you might think I'm biased in recommending the services of a professional. In reality, my reasons for making this recommendation are completely objective. The benefits are simply too plentiful and valuable to ignore. Don't take my word for it. Recent research by the Centre for Interuniversity Research and Analysis on Organizations (CIRANO) suggests that when two otherwise identical households — one working with a financial planner and one without — the family working with an advisor for a period of four to six years, accumulates 58 percent more.[1]

The following are the benefits a financial planner offers:

- Helps you to establish realistic goals.
- Creates a comprehensive financial plan outlining the action steps required to achieve your goals.
- Provides tax-savvy saving ideas.
- Protects you from financial risk with solid insurance advice and products.
- Provides you with solid investment advice ensuring a well-diversified investment portfolio.
- Works with the other professionals on your parent's team as needed, such as the accountant, banker, lawyer, or mortgage broker, helping your parent achieve optimal results.
- Helps you find suitable expertise if you do not already work with other professionals.
- Frees up your time, allowing you to focus on your own area of expertise or to spend your leisure time doing something you enjoy.

Similar to a personal fitness trainer, hiring a financial planner to coach you requires commitment on your part. A personal fitness trainer can tell you what exercises to do, but if you forget to do them, or you eat burgers and fries every night for dinner, you'll never achieve the best results. The financial planner's professional advice will be of little value if you are not prepared to follow through and implement the action steps he or she provides.

In addition to finding someone with qualifications and integrity, there are other things to consider when choosing the person who is best suited to work with you and your parents. Review Worksheet 13 to help you identify who you need on your team.

---

1 "The True Value of Advice," the *National Post*, October 13, 2012. Accessed January 29, 2014.

If your answers in Worksheet 13 show that you are worried about how to pay your parents' debts, you (or the power of attorney) should book an appointment with the credit manager at your parents' bank. Having an honest discussion about their ability to meet their debt obligations will put their banker or credit card company in a better position to help you restructure their loans. If this is not possible, you may need the services of a credit-counseling agency that will provide advice on how to manage bills and debts.

If you notice you have insurance concerns, then a life- and health-insurance agent will be necessary to help protect your parents from risk. As you saw in Chapter 8 on insurance, this advisor provides expert advice and offers health, life, and disability insurance as well as savings products such as annuities, variable annuities, guaranteed investment certificates (GICs), and mutual funds. Since new retirees and the elderly may have a need for critical illness and/or long-term care insurance, agents are experts that you need on your team. Many have their Certified Financial Planner (CFP) designation and are happy to prepare a comprehensive financial plan providing advice on both insurance and investments as part of their service. Since this type of advisor offers a broad range of products, they are often willing to work with small accounts. Life insurance advisors are generally paid a commission for selling you a product.

For basic tax-saving ideas, the services of a CFP can be useful. For more in-depth tax advice and preparation of your tax returns, your parent will need the services of a tax planner or a chartered accountant (CA).

If your parents' financial and tax affairs are simple, you may choose to complete their tax returns with the help of a software program, or you may engage the services of a tax preparation firm. If your parents' affairs are complex, you would be wise to hire an accountant to assist you with tax planning and the completion of your parents' tax return. Using an accountant can save you many dollars in taxes each year. You will pay either a set fee negotiated in advance for the service delivered, or an hourly rate billed after the service is complete. To avoid any unpleasant surprises, be sure to ask for an estimate in advance. Compensation should not be based on the size of the tax refund.

Worksheet 13
What Type of Advisor Does Your Parent Need?

1. **Debt:** I am worried about my parent's ability to pay his or her debt (e.g., mortgage, consumer loans, credit cards). *Answer yes or no.*

2. **Insurance Benefits:** *Add a checkmark to one or more of the following statements:*

   ☐ My parent's past employer offers a comprehensive health- and disability-insurance program, but I do not fully understand it.

   ☐ I worry about my parent's ability to care for himself or herself in the event of further illness or disability.

   ☐ I worry about the effect of taxation on my parent's estate.

   ☐ My parent is currently the caregiver for another dependent (e.g., spouse).

3. **Goal Planning:** *Add a checkmark to one of the following statements:*

   ☐ My parent has clear goals for the next five to ten years and has established a savings and investment plan to meet those goals.

   ☐ My parent needs help setting realistic goals and the strategies required to meet them.

4. **Budget:** I need help creating a budget for my parent and to help him or her stick to it. *Answer yes or no.*

5. **Savings:** *Add a checkmark to one of the following statements:*

   ☐ My parent has some savings, but I am unsure of which existing investments I should choose from to meet his or her income needs, and what additional investments to choose that will help him or her meet future goals.

   ☐ My parent is having trouble sticking to a savings plan.

6. **Taxes:** I am interested in learning how to reduce my parent's taxes. *Answer yes or no.*

7. **Real Estate:** My parent will likely need to sell the family home in the next five to ten years and he or she will need to use the proceeds from that sale, along with other savings, to create additional income for his or her elder years. *Answer yes or no.*

4. Choosing Your Team of Advisors

When looking for a financial planner or an advisor, you want someone you can relate to, and someone who understands your parents and their goals. Speaking to your friends and family may help you to identify the advisors they enjoy working with and provide you with some excellent recommendations.

You will want to hire the person with the best qualifications and reputation. You can check the professional standings of advisors you are interested in by going to websites for any associations to which they belong. Each advisor is part of a licensing regulatory body. Ask which professional association your potential advisor is affiliated with, and do an online search.

Take the time to interview at least three advisors for each area (e.g., accountants, lawyers, financial planners). This will allow you to compare each advisor and find the one who best understands your goals, demonstrates an understanding of the issues you and your elderly parents are facing, and is willing to count you among his or her valued clients. Book the interview appointment in their office, rather than in your home, as this will give you the opportunity to see how professional the office environment is.

Once you have chosen your advisory team, you will need to be ready to work with them by providing timely information. Arrive at meetings on time and prepared for the day's agenda. Ask lots of questions and bring a notepad to take notes so you can avoid follow-up questions and calls later. Tax, estate, and financial planning can be very complex and your advisor is there to simplify the process, provide clarity, and give you peace of mind. If you are unsure of a recommendation or product, keep asking questions until you understand exactly how implementing his or her recommendations will bring you closer to your goals. Don't be embarrassed by asking questions. You're not expected to be an expert.

When dealing with your advisors, you will find there is a lot of paperwork. Try not to feel rushed. Take your time, and ask your professional to take the time to go through the paperwork with you, explaining what you do not understand. If he or she is not prepared to do so, take the documents home where you can read them in peace, make notes, and return with a list of questions. Never sign a document you have not read or you do not understood!

Your relationship with your advisors will last many years when the lines of communication are kept open. Your advisor is your coach, showing the way to achieve your goals. You can count on him or her to keep you focused and on track.

When talking to these professionals, be assertive enough to ask some pointed questions about their experience and expertise. You want to be sure that they have a history of dealing with the issues you and your parents are facing. Worksheet 14 includes sample questions that will help you get the answers you need. You may want to print a few copies of this worksheet from the download kit so you have one for each type of advisor that you interview.

5. Regular Checkups

Just like the vehicle you drive, your parents' financial plan will require a regular checkup. Your financial planner will most likely suggest an annual review. Your planner will likely want to review the following questions with you:

- Have there been any changes in your parents' health or lifestyle that may impact their finances?

- Have their goals changed? If so, how?

- Will they be making a major purchase in the next year that will impact their cash flow?

- Are they able to stick to their budget?

- Have they been able to keep their savings on track to meet those goals?

- Have you and your parents been satisfied with the services you have been receiving from the planner?

Your financial planner will more than likely share ideas that can save your parents money on taxes. He or she will also review their health, disability, and life insurance needs at your annual meeting as well as review their investments and make recommendations for rebalancing their portfolio as required.

At your annual meeting you should ask your advisor the questions in Worksheet 15.

Over time you and your parents' financial planner will come to know each other very well. The better you know each other, the better your financial planner will understand your parents' goals and provide the coaching you need to achieve those goals. Many financial planners measure the success of their client relationships by their longevity. Your planner is in it for the long term and should do his or her best to see you succeed.

Worksheet 14
Questions to Ask Your Advisors

When you are interviewing financial planners, the following list of questions will help you gain a solid understanding of their abilities and the way they provide their services. These questions are equally applicable when looking for a lawyer or an accountant. Make sure the answers to these questions feel right to you. If they don't, keep looking.

1. What is your educational background?

2. What professional designations do you have?

3. How long have you been doing this job?

4. Has a complaint ever been lodged against you?

5. What percentage of your clients is elderly?

6. Without sharing confidential names or personal details, can you tell me about a time when you have helped resolve a challenging family situation involving the elderly?

7. Can you tell me about an experience you've had where you had to deal with multiple powers of attorney or siblings who disagreed about how to move forward?

8. How long would I expect to wait to have a call returned if I have questions?

9. Will we be working with you personally all the time? Or will we be working with one of your associates?

10. How often should I expect to meet with you?

11. Will any decisions be made without my knowledge or express consent?

12. Can I expect to receive a written plan or document outlining the goals we set and how we will reach them? Do you have an example of one you can show me?

13. How often should I expect to hear from you with updates or other information?

14. How are you paid (e.g., hourly, commission, fee-based)?

15. Are you offered additional financial incentives by your company, or by a third party, for recommending and selling any products?

16. What fees would be involved if I were to ever switch to another service provider if our relationship isn't providing what I need?

Worksheet 15
Annual Meeting Questions for the Advisor

1. Based on my parents' goals as described to you, how are we doing?

2. What more do we need to do to achieve these goals? What could we be doing better?

3. Why are you recommending this particular insurance or investment?

4. How does your recommendation (insurance or investment) meet my parents' goals?

5. Are there other choices that would help us reach those goals?

6. What, if any, are the costs to my parents if we implement your recommendation, both now and in the future?

7. Can we get our money back if needed? What if we need it sooner or change our mind?

8. How has this investment performed in the past? Is it realistic to expect the same performance in the future?

9. What are the risks involved with following, or not following, your recommendations?

Conclusion

Congratulations! You've made it through the book, and you're truly on your way to setting up yourself and your aging parents for financial success. Take a moment to feel good about all the work you have done to get the information you need for the future. I hope you feel prepared and empowered with the knowledge and resources I've given you to make this challenging time easier and less overwhelming.

Let's revisit Grace one last time and let you know how things are going now for her. At our first annual review, Grace and her daughters were still not ready to move Grace to a retirement facility. She would continue to live on her own for one more year. She was able to do so with the help of friends who would drive her to her various social functions and other appointments. Grace has a large group of friends from her book and theater clubs, and she continues to this day to attend the theater with those friends, and to read voraciously. Of course, she does not recall all that she reads anymore. When she was healthier, she used to love to travel, but cut back to day trips, accompanied by friends.

At the following year's financial review, the daughters and Grace were now ready to have Grace move into facility care. During the meeting, we discussed the sale of her home, and the selection of a retirement residence. I updated her cash flow statements to ensure this new lifestyle would be sustainable, and built in contingencies for increased care costs as her health deteriorates. I updated her investment portfolio to reflect the need for cash flow.

Grace is in good financial shape because of all the work she and her daughters have done, and are doing, and she is happy in her new assisted-care home, living comfortably and well in a studio suite.

It is probably safe to say that if you have read along with us to this final chapter, you too are going through a caregiving experience. From my own personal experience, I can tell you that this will be one of the most challenging times in your life. The good news is that you do not have to face it all on your own; there is help available. My experiences with the professionals who choose to work with the elderly are nothing short of amazing! Where do they find the patience and good grace to manage both aging parents and children's fears of the unknown with such goodwill?

Once you embark on this new journey, you will discover, as I did, what my father meant when he used to say to his children, "Life: It is not about you!" My dad was right, life is not about what we receive, it is about what we give.

Unlike our *net worth*, which is a simple mathematical measurement, our *self-worth* is a complex measurement of how we feel about ourselves when we look through the eyes of those we love.

A trick I used when trying to decide on the best course of action for my aging parents was to ask myself the following questions:

- If my parents were to pass away tomorrow, would I have any regrets?
- Should I have done more?
- What if I had kept my life simple by turning a blind eye to the potential for abuse?
- Would I be confident that every step was taken to ensure their comfort and safety?

The second strategy I employed was to seek the truth; to ask the tough questions, even if I knew the answers would be hard to swallow. By doing this, I found I was better prepared for what was to come next so that I might put a plan of action into place while there was still time.

By taking on the care of your elderly parents, you will find your self-worth grow by leaps and bounds. One day you will look back without regret, knowing you did everything you could do to ensure your parents were safe and comfortable. As an added bonus, your children will witness how you loved and cared for your parents. This will become their template for how to care for you. Today is a good day to begin that dialogue, too.

Download Kit

Please enter the URL you see in the box below into your computer web browser to access and download the kit.

www.self-counsel.com/updates/financialcare/14forms.htm

The kit includes forms in MS Word and MS Excel formats so that you can edit them to meet your needs:

- Net Worth Statement
- Multi-Year Net Worth Tracker
- Cash Flow Statement
- Worksheet 1: Determine Your Readiness to be a Caregiver
- Worksheet 2: Retirement Readiness
- Worksheet 3: Questions to Ask Your Parents

- Worksheet 4: Five Wishes
- Worksheet 5: Financial Planning Preparation
- Worksheet 6: Reviewing Documents: Consider, Investigate, and Act
- Worksheet 7: Out-of-Pocket Expense Tracker
- Worksheet 8: Gathering Debt Information
- Worksheet 9: Building Your Parents' Self-Awareness That They Need Help
- Worksheet 10: Living at Home versus Retirement Residence
- Worksheet 11: Comparing Retirement Homes
- Worksheet 12: Questions to Ask a Realtor
- Worksheet 13: What Type of Advisor Does Your Parent Need
- Worksheet 14: Questions to Ask Your Advisors
- Worksheet 15: Annual Meeting Questions for the Advisor

A Special Invitation

Loyola Press invites you to become one of our Loyola Press Advisors! Join our unique online community of people willing to share with us their thoughts and ideas about Catholic life and faith. By sharing your perspective, you will help us improve our books and serve the greater Catholic community.

From time to time, registered advisors are invited to participate in online surveys and discussion groups. Most surveys will take less than ten minutes to complete. Loyola Press will recognize your time and efforts with gift certificates and prizes. Your personal information will be held in strict confidence. Your participation will be for research purposes only, and at no time will we try to sell you anything.

Please consider this opportunity to help Loyola Press improve our products and better serve you and the Catholic community. To learn more or to join, visit **www.SpiritedTalk.org** and register today.

—The Loyola Press Advisory Team